Agile

Accidental ^ Project Manager

GROUP

Agile

Accidental ^ Project Manager
From Zero to Hero in 7 Iterations

Ray W. Frohnhoefer, MBA, PMP, CCP

Accidental Agile Project Manager: From Zero to Hero in 7 Iterations

ISBN-13: 978-0-9893770-9-6 (paperback)
ISBN-13: 978-1-7356213-0-2 (e-book)

Cover design by Luisito C. Pangilinan
Copyediting aided by Microsoft Word, Grammarly, and Hemingway Editor
References supported by Zotero
Indexing supported by DEXter by the Editorium

For more information about copyright or purchase, contact:

PPC Group, LLC
3450 3rd Avenue
Suite 309
San Diego, CA 92103 USA

https://ppcgroup.us
https://accidentalpm.online
http://rayfrohnhoefer.com

"Being a hero is no accident!" In his latest book, *"Accidental Agile Project Manager,"* Ray shares the backstory of Siwan Sero. Each chapter conveys the reality and essence of the "PROJECT" method. She needs to become a hero leading agile projects with the astute advice to *"embrace the accident...someone is counting on you."* This book is chock-full of tips, "knowledge nuggets," and training resources, and belongs on every new agile project manager's desk.

—Naomi Caietti
Author, Transform Your Project Leadership!
Managing Director, Naomi Caietti Consulting
Folsom, California

Ray has combined his extensive project management experience and expertise with a bestselling novelist's story-telling style to create a must-read for any accidental or aspiring agile project manager.

— Inham Hassen
PPM Trainer,
Features Editor - Mensa World Journal
United Kingdom

Thanks, Ray, for allowing me to review *Accidental Agile Project Manager*. Ray, you have done a great job with this book. I like the conversational style you have used in the book to present agile project management's fundamental concepts. It is easy to read and understand. Yes, this is truly meant for accidental agile project managers. Great work!

—Sumith Kahanda, Ph.D., M.SC., P.Eng., PMP, CSSGB
Project Manager, SaskWater
Saskatoon, Canada

About the Author

Ray Frohnhoefer is the Managing Partner of PPC Group, LLC, helping aspiring, new, and accidental project managers improve project management practice. Products and services include international bestsellers in Business Project Management, education, corporate training, and consulting.

Ray has led consulting teams in many industries and locations over his 40-year career. Notable projects include:

- rolling out of a UNIX development environment to 400+ developers in 16 locations
- testing electronic voting equipment with a team of 30 for San Diego County
- patenting an estimating tool used by a global Project Management Office.

No stranger to virtual, global teams, he has been working with and leading them his entire career.

Ray has had a dual career in project management and training. For eight years, he was an author, editor, and lecturer for the Edison Engineering Advanced Course in Computers. He has been teaching project management and business analysis classes for UC San Diego Extension for 18 years.

A long-time Project Management Institute (PMI) volunteer, Ray served as President of the PMI San Diego Chapter in 2005. In 2006 he was the first official PMI Region Mentor for Southwest North America. He has supported several international PMI committees and groups over the past 15 years. He currently serves as a member of the PMI Ethics Review Committee. Ray also helped the PMI Educational Foundation create its first professional development scholarship, and he continues to support their work.

Ray holds an undergraduate degree in Mathematics with a concentration in Computer Science and an MBA degree in Technology Management. He is a PMI Leadership Institute Masters Class graduate and a Certified Computer Professional (CCP).

Dedication

I dedicate this book to:

- my parents, who encouraged a love of reading and writing at an early age

- my husband, who provided unconditional love and support for this project

- my learners and clients, who always inspire me

- my muses, Hope and S'mores, for all the inspirational petting and snack breaks

- aspiring, new, and accidental project managers everywhere - you rock!

—Ray

Table of Contents

List of Figures and Tables

Foreword by Jorge Valdés Garciatorres

When I was in the Project Management Institute's Leadership Institute Master Class with Ray and two other colleagues, we decided to do a team presentation. The activity would allow us to continue to work together after the class and create a presentation to help other PMI leaders. As strategic leaders, each of us had something to say, and soon we were in the team "storming" phase almost without noticing.

All of us were leaders, and each had their own opinion. Just as we were about to give up, Ray asked us to have a retrospective of what we had done so far.

Thanks to Ray's good advice, we became aware of what was happening to us. He suggested that together we analyze the work at hand, identify the tasks we had to perform, and provide the final deliverable. As a team, we decided how to split the work and defined the standards we would meet. In the end, we worked in pairs, and we finished ahead of time. An earlier finish gave us some time to share a couple of beers while we rehearsed what we were going to present at the next meeting.

That night, after recapping my day, I realized that Ray has acted like a … let's say, Scrum Master. He facilitated decision-making, honored the team's wisdom, kept us on track, and helped us become a better performing team. I realized how much I had enjoyed our time working together as a team.

In 2018, Ray kindly accepted my offer to collaborate with him on his book on project management. When I read the book, I enjoyed the way Ray presented the essentials of project management. It was, and still is, a great book.

When he contacted me to be part of this second project, I was eager to review the manuscript. He has now made agile easier for an aspiring or entry-level project manager.

He has done it again! Ray has mastered the skill of explaining complicated subjects and making them easy to understand and practice. I have read the new manuscript twice, and I found that Ray not only explains agile project management, but he practices it in his work. This book you are about to read has had several iterations of expert review. It improved significantly from one iteration to another.

I congratulate Ray on this new milestone achieved. I encourage you to use this book as a companion for your agile projects. I am sure that, as we explain at the beginning, Ray will help you too.

— **Jorge Valdés Garciatorres, PMP**
Ciudad de México
September 2020

Foreword by John Estrella

My project management career started by accident, which is probably similar to how other project managers began their careers. While some five-year-olds may aspire to become a doctor, lawyer, astronaut, or some other profession, I have yet to hear someone seek project management as a career, even while they are in college. It's usually the project management career that finds them. That's why Ray's initial book, *Accidental Project Manager,* filled a much-needed void in the profession.

You'll hear the story of "zero to hero" repeated in various industries. A good programmer may be asked to lead a small team. Later, the same programmer will be given a title, such as a project leader. Before you know it, that title will morph into project manager. A similar story can happen to an executive assistant who may be asked to organize a corporate retreat. A few months later, the same person may be managing multiple events and be given a formal project management title. Likewise, a social worker may end up managing several fundraising projects. Without formal project management training, they find themselves in a precarious situation. They need something to start their projects correctly … and they need to do it quickly!

Reading a hard-to-decipher body of knowledge or taking a course in school takes too long. When Ray approached me in 2018 about addressing this gap, I suggested a simple process to help accidental project managers go from zero to hero within a week. Coincidentally, the word PROJECT is seven letters, so we came with an acronym to help new project managers remember the process: People, Requirements, Organize, Jell, Execute, Control, and Transfer. That's how the PROJECT Method was born.

Admittedly, I was really impressed with how Ray crafted a compelling story to introduce the concepts. It made reading the book engaging and easy to understand. Trust me; you'd rather read his initial book instead of a project management standard.

His initial book focused on traditional project management. For someone new, it's an excellent starting point. However, there is a momentous shift to agile project management. Somewhere in between is a hybrid approach- a mix of traditional, incremental, iterative, and agile. This new book, *Accidental Agile Project Manager: Zero to Hero in 7 Iterations*, closes the gap between predictive and adaptive project management while leveraging the simplicity of his initial book.

If you are new to agile, the number of providers and their competing certifications can be overwhelming. To avoid the confusion, Ray aligned this book with the *PMBOK® Guide* and the *Agile Practice Guide*. He made some difficult choices to reconcile the differences from various sources and presented concepts and terms which are generally accepted, most of the time, regardless of the industry. In the end, he managed to deliver a concise introduction to help accidental agile project managers become successful in their first few projects. In doing so, he's enabling you to shed your "accidental" title to that of a seasoned agile project manager.

As you go through this book, remember that people power projects. You need to dig for requirements and organize the objectives. The project team has to jell so that they can execute the activities effortlessly. As a project manager, control casually and transfer the project by transforming it into operational work. These are the same concepts in a predictive project environment, with some processes adjusted to address adaptive projects' unique approach.

Embrace your new role as an agile project manager. With this book, it will be exhilarating!

— **John A. Estrella, PhD, CMC, PMP**
Ontario, Canada
September 2020

Preface

It was the fall of 2014, and I was teaching for a 120-hour state-approved project management course. The class was attended by aspiring, new, and accidental project managers. They worked in non-profits and for-profits in industries such as technology, construction, and healthcare.

I love teaching project management and wanted to see everyone succeed. Many former employees and students are now corporate vice presidents and business owners.

I could tell some advanced topics were way too confusing. Some had received promotions for taking the class, so excitement for hours of advanced subject matter material was low. When meeting students after the course, I found their retention of materials was also low.

The *PMBOK® Guide – Sixth Edition*, with the *Agile Practice Guide*, contains over 800 pages of information and standards (or three times the size of the Third Edition) is no longer a good book for beginners. There is way too much material to learn, absorb, and put into regular practice in a short time. A lot of the course material I had to present would have no immediate use. I re-drafted my content to add more useful information and remove as much advanced content as I could.

I realized I could offer students what they needed - just enough project management to get started. I reviewed skill lists and selected the smallest useful set. With the help of my business mentor, Dr. John Estrella, *Accidental Project Manager: Zero to Hero in 7 Days* and the PROJECT method were born.

After reaching the top of Amazon's bestselling lists, my phone started ringing. There was a demand for a course based on the book. I pulled together the modules and started delivering classroom training to rave reviews. My clients included local governments, organizations, and the US Navy. But there was still a problem.

While the book was selling globally, the classroom training was confined to a region and small groups. My work was not finished yet.

Using my classroom content, I created *Accidental Project Manager: The Online Experience*, which goes beyond the book. With a week of study, a new project manager should get on the right path, with less stress for current projects and no stress from advanced topics.

The original book and course focused on the traditional "waterfall" project management. With a set of content for predictive projects, I could now concentrate on iterative projects. The same class that inspired the original book also had a unit of materials on agile. It allowed me to study learner needs for agile projects and project management.

One of the problems I faced in writing this book was that agile experts kept throwing out terms that I should be including. Unfortunately, agile project management is a lot less mature and developed than "traditional" or "waterfall" project management. There are 50+ forms of agile identified so far, and the terminology among them is not shared or standardized. Two people told me I had to include the term "backlog grooming." The three significant standards for agile and agile project management that I used did not include it.

As before, the book and course do not try to teach everything about agile projects. It contains essential information extracted from three major agile project management standards and some other practices that are generally accepted in agile forms. The content is aligned with PMI's *PMBOK® Guide* and *Agile Practice Guide* and the PMI-ACP (Agile Certified Practitioner) certification topics.

I hope you enjoy and learn from this book and have as much fun with your careers as the team and I have. Like Siwan Sero, I encourage you to be positive and become the heroes of your projects. Be sure to start your learning journey now!

— Ray W. Frohnhoefer
San Diego, California

Acknowledgments

There were so many people involved with this book that the best way to start is, "I'm sorry if I've left out your name."

First, I'd like to thank Dr. John Estrella. John is an excellent business coach and mentor – all of us who work with him have experienced impressive business transformations. Without John's guidance, this book would probably not be written. John also wrote a foreword for the book.

A big thank you to my friend and PMI colleague, Jorge Valdes Garciatorres, for again writing the foreword. Jorge's stories also help to make the material more memorable and relatable.

Also, Luis Pangilinan has done fabulous work on all our covers, and this one is no exception.

I also want to acknowledge Tim Fitzpatrick of Rialto Marketing for assistance with clarity for the marketing of the book, course, and other PPC Group products.

Next, I'd like to thank the many global professionals who have helped in many ways, including reading, editing, and giving feedback and guidance: Charles Adams, Mahfooz Ali, Upendra Babu, Shweta Brahmakshatriya, Naomi Caietti, John Estrella, Jorge Valdes Garciatorres, Murray Grooms, Inham Hassen, Sumith Kahanda, Nitin Kundeshwar, Rajendra Matlani, Venkata Pegatraju, Sandra Rowe, Sanjay Sengupta, Harjit Singh, and Kashif Zafeer. Your inputs and insights have been invaluable. Their ideas have helped to ensure the material is appropriate for a global audience.

I'd also like to thank the staff at California Southern University and UC San Diego Extension for their encouragement and support of this project.

And finally, I'd like to thank the many folks that follow me on social media: Facebook (including Groups PM360 and Project Manager, and the Project Management Page), LinkedIn, Twitter, Instagram, and YouTube. Your encouragement shaped many topics, and the tips and "nuggets" included at the end of each chapter.

#ACCIDENTALAGILEPM

INTRODUCTION: BECOME A PROJECT HERO

What's an accidental project manager, you ask? Anyone who suddenly and unexpectedly finds themselves responsible for a project. Maybe the home remodel project turned out to be a little more complicated and complex than you expected. An organization you volunteer for may need a plan to build a new wing for an orphanage and asks you to help. Or your manager gave you a project management textbook and put you in charge of an important work project. In business, it is not uncommon to see team leaders doing project managers' work, and they may not even be aware.

Congratulations, you just became an accidental project manager!

This book is the missing project management "quick start" guide for accidental project managers assigned to agile projects. Agile projects are those with repeated life cycles. Detailed requirements are determined and approved before each iteration, which results in a deliverable.

What happens in most cases is that accidental project managers fail, and only then seek out training. Sometimes, if they are fortunate, they get the support of their employer. Usually, they just don't know where to begin. Often the culture of their organization doesn't offer sufficient support.

Many also aren't sufficiently prepared to absorb all the knowledge of even a primary project management curriculum. Most could benefit from the information contained in this book – a quick set of basics they can learn in a short period to improve their early project experiences.

Accidental project managers come from all walks of life. They include employees with industry or subject matter expertise, those who may be in career transition, and transitioning military service members. They are also not specific to any particular culture – accidental project managers exist in any geographical location where project managers are found.

Here's a brief profile of the typical accidental project manager:

- Age is the mid-20s to mid-30s (and up, there is no real age limit)
- Develops expertise in their industry – they are subject matter experts (SMEs) working their way up the ranks
- Has little to no formal project management training
- Often receives little or no organizational support for training, coaching, or mentoring
- Has excellent interpersonal skills, demonstrates leadership through work on projects as a team member, or owns their own business
- Starts with vital, yet smaller to medium-sized projects with smaller teams – the work often isn't referred to as a project; however, it has the hallmarks of a project

The best advice: embrace the accident! Perhaps the most important reason is that *someone is counting on you.* Your spouse doesn't want to live in an unfinished home for years. Your organization needs to control costs while advancing its mission. Your manager most likely selected you because there were no other candidates. So, clear your mind of those self-doubts – be positive and give it your best effort. You can do this!

Even the most seasoned professionals have been accidental project managers at some points in their careers. Someone trained as a software project manager may know nothing about hiring and budgets when they remodel their home basement. These may be unused project skills due to the nature of the work projects they manage.

Suppose you can create project templates and methodologies that executives and teams want. In that case, you may find yourself promoted to a Project Management Office position. There you will work closely with project managers, supporting them with templates, training, and consulting. You aren't the first, and you won't be the last, accidental project manager.

Embrace your status as an accidental project manager because this is your opportunity to explore exciting new career opportunities. Career opportunities such as these are not just where you currently reside, but available globally. Estimates suggest that employers will need to fill 2.2 million project management and project management-related positions annually from 2017 through 2027.

The career is financially rewarding as well – project manager compensation is 82% higher than non-project management roles on the average (Anderson Economic Group, 2017). There's never been a more exciting time to explore the career potential of project management.

Let's start by making sure you are working on a project. A project is:

- A temporary set of activities with a distinct beginning and end date
- Activities which intend to produce a new and unique product, service, or other result

The project manager is comparable to an orchestra conductor. A project manager uses resources (people, equipment, and material), applies tools and skills, and orchestrates the resources to produce the project result. The project manager is familiar with the entire score and knows how each activity contributes to the final symphony.

PROJECT VS. OPERATION

A project is distinct from "operations" since it produces something new and unique instead of making something repeatedly, perhaps with only small refinements or changes.

Examples of projects include:

- Remodel a kitchen
- Design and build a new home
- Develop, market, and sell a new online course
- Create a new audio guide service for a museum
- Purchase and install new computer hardware systems
- Merge two or more entities after an acquisition

Project

- Unique Output
- Temporary
- Expends budget to produce result

Operation

- Ongoing and repetitive output
- More or less permanent
- Needs to be profitable

The fellow who claims he manages seventy-two projects every week by mixing custom chemical reagents isn't leading a project. He is essentially repeating the same necessary steps seventy-two times and earning a profit for his company. The repeated measures are a process. If he wants to increase his throughput to 100 shipments per week, that might need a project.

There is a process and an acronym to help the accidental project manager remember all projects' necessary steps. It's Ray's **PROJECT** method:

People
Requirements
Organize
Jell
Execute
Control
Transfer

The purpose of the PROJECT method is to get you started quickly, not make you an expert or teach you everything you need to know. This book is written as a business story to help deliver this message. It follows the method as a fictional person applies it to a realistic but imaginary organizational scenario. This approach makes the character and the process more relatable and memorable to the reader.

The PROJECT method is versatile and applicable to a variety of different types of projects and project life cycles. In *Accidental Project Manager*, we saw how Rhett Sero managed a project using a traditional method known as predictive or "waterfall." This name was given because the activities of the project are linear and cascade into one another. This life cycle has a focus on managing costs. In this book, we'll see how Rhett's cousin, Siwan, applies the PROJECT method to a form of project management that has evolved for projects with adaptive or agile[1] life cycles.

Life Cycle	Use to	Project Activities	Delivery
Predictive	Control costs and manage change	Performed once	Single
Incremental	Complete project faster	Performed for each increment	Frequent, small
Iterative	Assure scope and correctness	Repeated until correct	Single
Agile	Provide client value and get feedback for improvement	Perform until correct	Frequent, small

Table 1: Four Major Life Cycle Categories

The critical difference is that agile projects produce deliverables over multiple iterations; detailed requirements are determined and approved before each iteration. The benefit of the approach is that clients often have early access to some project deliverables. The project team gets early feedback for improvement. Clients also receive the highest value deliverables first, so they may even realize a more rapid investment return.

It is essential to understand what we mean by "agile" more precisely. It all started with "Agile" (with a capital "A"). I generally refer to Agile as meaning the Agile Manifesto, a document produced in 2001 to detail a different way to develop software.

Agile, in its purest form, did not require project management. Agile was meant to be practiced by self-organizing teams.

---

[1] Agile life cycles are a combination of two other life cycles – iterative and incremental. With these definitions in mnd, it is important for the project manager to choose a life cycle aligned with project success factors.

Unfortunately, the idea of continuous development with unlimited resources and time isn't a reality for most organizations. Senior executives need budgets, schedules, and more for sound decision-making. Hence, over time, the concept of "agile" (with a lower case "a") projects emerged.

While agile projects still draw many of their values from Agile, they generally share a different set of values than predictive or "waterfall" projects. These values are derived from the Agile Manifesto (Beck, 2001):

Agile Values	Waterfall Values[2]	What it Means
Individuals and interactions	Process and tools	Agile projects are more collaborative.
Demonstrated results	Comprehensive documentation	Agile projects focus on making iterative deliveries of a working product.
Client collaboration	Contract negotiation	Initial requirements are less detailed. The client is represented on project teams and works day-by-day to define the product.
Responding to change	Following a plan	New requirements are acceptable and welcome at any time.

Table 2: Waterfall vs. Agile Values

Some examples of agile life cycle projects include:

- An educational software package developed in smaller components over time to incorporate end-user feedback in the final product

---

[2] Waterfall values are inferred from Agile values, but were never formally stated.

- A music playing application that needs to get something in place quickly to remain competitive, and then improve the product over time
- A TV station producing several small, inexpensive pilot programs and testing them with audiences before deciding which programs to air
- A company taking steps to transition from a conglomerate to a financial services company

There are many different "flavors" of agile projects which have emerged, including Scrum, Kanban, XP (Extreme Programming), and Disciplined Agile (DA). At last count, there were more than 50. In this book, we're not going to assume any specific form of agile. Instead, we're going to examine core values and essentials which are a part of almost every project with an agile life cycle and adopted by the most well-known agile methods.

As mentioned, the idea of continuous development with unlimited resources and time isn't a reality for most organizations. Senior executives need budgets, schedules, and more for sound decision-making. As such, I've learned that using some basic project management practices will help.

With these reasonable compromises, the PROJECT method works equally well for waterfall and agile life cycles, with some modest differences in some of the steps. Agile life cycles are no longer just for software development – they have been adopted in many industries, including construction, manufacturing, and healthcare.

Each chapter is devoted to a step of the method and ends with "Knowledge Nuggets" – tips, basic templates, and references for further reading and study. References include sections of the *Agile Practice Guide*, a document chartered by both the Project Management Institute (PMI) and the Agile Alliance®.

Agile Requires	What Works
Done when done	Time boxes – within x amount of time
Change at any cost	Cost boxes – within x dollars
Incremental delivery	Release and iteration planning
Self-organizing teams	A collaboration of coach, product owner, and team to identify the best resources to complete tasks; the project manager as a servant leader
Conversations and collaboration	Information captured and posted in addition to daily meetings
Team co-location	Core time together and remote work arrangements
Client a part of the team	Core time together and remote work arrangements

Table 3: What Works for Agile

Where content for general project management skills applicable for all life cycles is necessary, these are taken from the *PMBOK® Guide – Sixth Edition*, PMIs standard for project management. PMI has indicated this information will also carry forward into future editions.

All PMI standards are both flexible and non-prescriptive. They rely heavily on practitioners to interpret the standards and apply them to their specific project circumstances. What is captured in this book is the collective wisdom of "what works" for accidental agile project managers on their early project assignments.

Please read the "backstory" of Siwan Sero, our accidental agile project manager, and to-be hero. Follow Siwan as she prepares to manage her first agile project. Each chapter after this represents one of the seven iterations of her learning of the PROJECT method.

Backstory: Siwan Sero

Siwan Sero, a cousin of Rhett Sero, is another talented software developer for the Xanadu Partnership, a small San Diego software development company of about 100 employees. Siwan followed in her cousin's footsteps and just finished another critical software application for the Washington Corporation (WashCo).

Both her manager and client were ecstatic with the result. Siwan threw every ounce of her energy into the product – she loved her work. And like her cousin, when others on the development team got stuck and were unable to complete their work, she quietly and efficiently helped them succeed. Her passion for the job and leadership of the development team did not go unnoticed.

One Friday afternoon, as the project was winding down, Dennis, her manager, summoned her to his office. "Siwan, I can't stress enough how thrilled WashCo and Xanadu are with your project results. Not only did you complete a project that exceeded client expectations, but you also demonstrated significant leadership through your work with your peers."

"Thank you, sir," Siwan replied sheepishly, "I enjoyed the project immensely."

"Siwan, your good work did not go unnoticed. Movie Vault, a start-up classical movie streaming service, has been on our sales radar for six months. They want to get a web application up and running quickly, something basic to start with and expandable with more features. They value the flexibility to make changes to meet the needs of their customers. We're confident you can lead the project."

"I'm sure I can, sir," Siwan replied. "I just need a few more weeks to wrap up some details."

"Unfortunately, after they heard about your success," Dennis continued, "we're unable to hold them off any longer. We need to start their project two weeks from Monday, and they expect that it will take about a year – there is some flexibility in the end date."

"But sir," Siwan said with some hesitation, "I'm not prepared to manage a project of this importance. I wouldn't know where to begin."

"That's OK, Siwan. Take the weekend to rest and give it some thought. On Monday morning, a project management consultant I hired for seven days will meet with you. He has a lot of project management knowledge and experience, especially with agile life cycle projects, and is as passionate about it as you are about your software development work. I trust he will be able to get you started in seven days so you can help Movie Vault achieve the same success as WashCo."

How could she rest? Siwan knew she had no clue how to manage projects – Dennis simply told her what needed to be done and by when. She had very little insight since she enjoyed working heads-down on her code. She would hardly rest that weekend as she somewhat dreaded what Monday would bring.

She never thought that she would end up being the hero of the story.

Knowledge Nuggets

Chapter Pro Tip: Begin with the end in mind; pick the right method.

When managing a project, it's best to start thinking about the end goal and the steps to reach it. Dennis helped set Siwan up for success. He quickly informed her of the critical project aspects. As you will see, this plays an important role later. One of the first and most important decisions to make is the type of life cycle to use.

Predictive or "waterfall" life cycles define the project as much as possible up front. Changes and costs require careful management. The early definition of requirements ensures deadlines and contractual obligations are achievable. If for any reason, they cannot be, there are usually early warning signs. These signs enable clients to make choices. Waterfall life cycles typically work best for projects with needs that can be well defined or have significant constraints.

Accidental project managers can benefit from encountering waterfall life cycles first. But there are times when other life cycles can be crucial.

In contrast, adaptive or "agile" life cycles iterate to achieve a less well-defined overall scope. The exact requirements and scope are defined and approved before each iteration. While essential needs may be known up front, details are apparent as the project moves forward.

Agile life cycles allow for scope flexibility and risk management. The flexibility often comes with a sacrifice of time and cost. The agile life cycle also works best for exploratory projects and projects requiring greater flexibility. In some cases, product feedback from the client may be essential to include as the project progresses.

Agile life cycles also provide an opportunity to enhance risk management for the project scope. With client involvement and incremental development, there is less risk of the project building something unnecessary.

Agile Practice Guide reading: Chapter 2 introduces agile. Chapter 3 discusses the pros and cons of each life cycle choice in more detail. The Annexes at the end of the guide show the relationships of Agile, agile, and other project management concepts.

PMBOK® Guide reading: Part I, Chapters 1-3 to learn more about projects and general project management.

Article: The accidental project manager (Hunsberger, 2011)

Blog Articles:
Plan projects like Albert Einstein (Frohnhoefer, 2019a)

You Know You are a "Knighted" Project Manager When ... (Frohnhoefer, 2020b)

CHAPTER 1

ITERATION 1: POWERED BY PEOPLE

As the weekend came to an end, Siwan could barely sleep. Sunday night, she kept wondering about who she would meet and what she would learn. Monday morning, Siwan arrived early, but someone had come earlier. She found her whiteboard divided into thirds. On the left, she saw:

---

4 Critical Tips to Succeed as a Project Manager

1. Clarify expectations
2. The importance of just enough planning
3. Ask a lot of questions and think before asking
4. Give trust to get trust

On the right side, she observed:

Projects Ultimately Succeed or Fail Because of People

- People are impacted by the project
- People are involved in the project as team members
- People act and make decisions which will impact the project
- Know these people – how they are impacted and how they work with the team.

And in the middle was an acrostic that spelled **PROJECT**:

People
Requirements
Organize
Jell with the Team
Execute
Control
Transfer

As she pondered the writing source, a cheerful voice emerged behind her and interrupted her thoughts: "Projects," Ms. Sero, "are powered by people. The P in the PROJECT method is for People."

She turned to notice a slight, gray-haired man with a sparkle in his eye was standing in her doorway. He was dressed in a sharp and conservative business suit that almost looked like a military uniform. The generational difference was evident. She immediately wondered how this man could teach her anything about project management for modern software development, or for that matter, for any projects.

16

Without giving Siwan a chance to say anything, he continued, "Without the right people involved, your project will be delayed at best, fail at worst. A project I recently reviewed experienced delays because someone impacted by the project wasn't consulted. The stakeholder found a way to keep it from moving forward for six months. Do you know who the right people are for your project, Ms. Sero?"

Sheepishly she shook her head no, still wondering who this was and how he appeared in her doorway so quickly. "Maybe I really should pay attention," she thought to herself. She knew that Dennis trusted this man, so maybe she should as well.

"Good. Think first and always ask questions. I'm Harry Heldenmacher, and you can call me Harry. You may recall that my wife, Heda, worked with your cousin Rhett. Heda is out of the country on another assignment, so I will work with you and give you some agile project management tips and techniques."

"We're going to spend the next seven working days iterating together, much like the iterations of an agile project. I'm going to make sure you succeed with the Movie Vault project by outlining the PROJECT method, one letter per iteration. We'll discuss the steps to take both before the project starts and when it is underway. I'll equip you with the basic tools to succeed."

"Each iteration, we will:

- review your progress,
- learn a new part of the PROJECT method,
- summarize what you learned, and
- have some overnight homework.

After that, it's up to you. Are you willing to work with me?"

Siwan relaxed and held out her hand, "Nice to meet you, Harry. I look forward to learning from you."

"The PROJECT method is where we begin. It represents the basic steps you need to take as a project manager of any project," Harry explained. "Before we do that, let's look at the four critical success tips."

Harry's success tips included four points:

1. Clarify expectations

    For this concept, Harry explained that Siwan needed to know what was committed to for the project and the expectations of Dennis (who was Siwan's manager and the project sponsor), the client, and others. Through the "Requirements" step in the PROJECT methodology, she would develop that understanding and make sure her team did. Everyone needs to be on the same page.

2. The importance of just enough planning

    "Einstein said that if he had sixty minutes to solve a problem, he would spend fifty-five minutes defining and understanding it. After that, he would spend five minutes solving it," stated Harry.

    "You need a similar approach with project planning – be sure you understand what needs to be done and plan the steps to get there before you start doing anything. While you won't necessarily spend more than 90% of the project time planning, the top project managers spend 91% more time planning than average project managers. Spending this extra time is important to practice from the start" (Crowe, 2006).

    "Agile projects may require a little less planning around scope due to how they are structured, but enough planning is still important. It's equally important to be able to decide when you have enough planning," Harry continued. "Don't get stuck in what's known as 'analysis paralysis' – plans are useless unless put into action."

3. Ask a lot of questions

"The third concept," Harry continued, "is to ask a lot of questions. Think first and use the facts at hand. There may be 'obvious' requirements, but do not make unfounded assumptions. Asking the right clarifying questions can save a project from failure. As they say, seek first to understand, then be understood."

4. Give trust to get trust

Harry explained that another essential concept was that Siwan should give trust first to get trust. "Don't assume anyone has any ill intent – this will allow you to build trust faster," Harry counseled. "Teamwork is smoother if everyone trusts everyone else to do their part. We'll examine this concept more on the fourth iteration when we focus on teamwork."

Harry then moved to the right third of the whiteboard, explaining that there are two main types of people involved in projects – those impacted by the project and those on the project team. Unlike Xanadu's waterfall project teams, the agile teams had three significant roles:

- **Team Facilitator**: The team facilitator for an agile project is a servant leader. Rather than direct work, the servant leader acts as a mentor and a coach, helps the team with planning and documentation responsibilities, and removes roadblocks. The team facilitator is also responsible for providing the project and progress information needed by Xanadu management.

- **Product Owner**: The product owner works with the team and other stakeholders to set the direction and provide the product's requirements. The product owner is responsible for prioritizing the work to ensure the team is always delivering the highest value features that meet the clients' needs and other stakeholders.

- **Cross-Functional Team Members**: Cross-functional team members come from multiple Xanadu business units. They must have the skills necessary to complete the project. These team members might include business analysts, designers and architects, developers, testers, and integrators for any project.

Harry further explained that for this project, Xanadu management had decided that:

- Siwan would assume the role of the team facilitator, in addition to being the project manager
- Movie Vault will provide the product owner
- Cross-functional team members would include:
    o A business analyst to assist the product owner and team facilitator
    o Developers
    o Testers

"Managing a cross-functional team typically increases the number of stakeholders. Since each cross-functional team member may report to a different functional manager, these managers are impacted by the project," continued Harry.

Siwan understood immediately. "That means Barbara, the BA Manager, Dennis, my manager, who is also the Development Manager, and Quincy, the QA Manager, are impacted by the project," she stated confidently.

Harry challenged Siwan to brainstorm a list of those that would be impacted by the project. This list would include Movie Vault management, Movie Vault clients, Xanadu management, and her peers. Next, they started to identify who had the most interest and power.

Jim, the Movie Vault Product Manager, had both power and interest since this was his project. The rest of the Movie Vault management team was divided, so they were named individually. Very quickly, the list grew to include over a dozen groups and nearly the same number of individual people.

Harry provided Siwan with a Stakeholder Register Template[3] to document her findings, explaining that "stakeholder" was used to describe all the people impacted by or involved in a project. He asked her to think more about it overnight and then share with her project team later – together, they would check to see if anyone was missing.

Name	Contact Information	Role	Project Phase	Requirements / Expectations	Internal/ External	Power	Interest
Jim	jim@m-vault.com	Client, Product Owner	All	Project delivered that delights customers	External	5	5
Dennis	dennis@xanadu.com	Project Sponsor	All	Bi-weekly status updates and 1-1 meeting, a project delivered that meet's Jim's approval	Internal	5	5
Siwan	siwan@xanadu.com	PM (me)	All	Conduct project per the PROJECT methodology	Internal	4	5
Xanadu Functional Managers	barbara@xanadu.com quincy@xanadu.com	Manage resources	All	Weekly status updates, monthly briefing about resource utilization	Internal	4	4
Movie Vault Content Team	Contact via Jim	Project end users	Planning (some), Transfer	Participate in project requirements elicitation and receive an excellent product that meets their needs; Jim will provide reports to them	External	3	4
Movie Vault Security Manager	security@m-vault.com	Project end user	Planning (some), Transfer	Participate in project requirements elicitation and receive an excellent product that meets their needs; Jim will provide reports to them	External	3	4
Movie Vault customers	Contact via Jim	Project end users	Transfer	Receive an excellent product that meets their needs; Jim will monitor for changes	External	3	1
...	...	...	...	...	...	...	...

Figure 1: Sample Stakeholder Register

---

[3] All templates illustrated in this book are accompanied by instructions and pre-filled examples. Please see the end material in this book to learn how to access and use them.

"It is always better to over-identify, rather than under identify stakeholders," continued Harry. "One can always pare it down later. You will need to share the stakeholders with Dennis, your manager. And for Dennis and everyone you share it with, ask two questions: 'Who else should I speak to about this project?' and 'Have I missed any important stakeholders?'"

Once satisfied that they identified most of the project's people, Harry turned Siwan's attention to the cross-functional team members. He explained that the best people to work on the team are those who:

- want to be there,
- have the skills to contribute to the project, and
- know of others who can help.

Why are these three attributes important? Those that want to be there will show up every day ready to do their best work. And of course, they must have the skills to do that work. Sometimes, the team may get "stuck" on difficult issues, and that's where "who" the team knows can help. The members of the team can reach out to those outside the organization for solutions.

"Siwan, project managers, especially on their first project, don't always pick their project team. However, I'd like you to think carefully about who would be best for your team. I'm going to talk to Dennis – while neither of us can make any promises, we want to hear your input."

"Communications is key," continued Harry, after they returned from lunch. "Project managers spend anywhere between 75-90% of their time communicating either formally or informally" (Haus, 2016). He explained how Siwan and her team would need to figure out what needed to be communicated. There are four "must-have" elements for facilitating project communications:

TOOLS FOR MESSAGING

1. Elevator Pitch: Short account of project and its value

2. Project Deck: Compilation of project slides

3. Status Report: Update on project progress

4. Communications Plan: What gets communicated to who, when, and by what method.

- Elevator pitch – this is a brief thirty-to-sixty second summary that describes the project objectives and its benefits. Use it to quickly relay information about the project to interested executives and others.

- Project deck – this is a compilation of all slides from previous presentations given on the project. Having the slide deck enables new slides to be quickly assembled when needed, increases consistency in communications, and instills confidence in the project.

- Status report – this is one or more simple reports containing project status information, tailored to the stakeholder audience. Harry suggested that a high-level status report be delivered every two weeks to Dennis to brief him on the project progress. Harry indicated they would look at this in more detail later. With an agile project, since the client or their representative is directly participating, they should know the status.

- Communications plan –this is an often overlooked, yet valuable document that outlines what project information would be shared, with whom, when, in what format, and at what frequency. Communication needs can be clarified with stakeholders during requirements identification and other planning activities.

Harry provided Siwan with a second template: a project Communications Plan Template. He asked her to add the status reports to the plan and then work with the team and client to determine what other vital communications would be required.

"During the Vietnam War," Harry explained, "Heda and I worked with Captain Grace Hopper. While she was excellent at getting what her team needed at the Pentagon, she angered some top brass. She didn't keep them well informed about the team's work; she failed to report to some of them and got others to work with her team without clearing it with anyone. There was no communications plan, and as a result, people felt left out."

Stakeholder	Information/Key Messages	Purpose	Method/ Format	Target Date/ Frequency	Responsible	Comments
Jim	Project Kickoff Meeting	Invitation	Email	One time – 7/18/18	Siwan	
Dennis	Weekly Status Report	Inform on progress	Emailed report	Bi-weekly (Mondays)	Siwan	May need additional reports for other stakeholders TBD
Team	Daily Stand Up Meeting	Inform on progress	Meeting	Daily (9 am)	Siwan	
Team	Retrospectives	Continuous Improvement	Meeting	At the end of every sprint	Siwan	
Team, Movie Vault TBD	Demo	Show tangible progress	Meeting	At the end of every sprint and the end of the project	Siwan	
Dennis	Weekly 1:1 Meeting	Review project issues	Face-to-face	Weekly (Fridays)	Siwan	Dennis will set up on the calendar
Pointeast Manager	Contract	Contract sign off	Email	One time	Siwan	When a contract is available

Figure 2: Sample Communications Plan

"As payback for the perceived exclusion, they purposely gave her team a computer without the capacity to run the software they knew her team had to write. It impacted team morale and slowed them down at a critical time. Her team and colleagues confronted her and begged her to change and find better ways to communicate."

"While she developed her communication skills, her team invented virtual memory to solve the limited computer problem. It delayed their project work by months, but their virtual memory solution became the basis for most modern computer operating systems."

"By doing a little more planning and communicating, Captain Hopper and her team completely turned the situation around to everyone's delight. Xanadu and Movie Vault are counting on you, Siwan, to have equal success."

As the day came ended, Harry summarized what they had covered that day:

Chapter Summary

- The PROJECT Method – P is for people
- Projects succeed or fail because of the actions taken and decisions made by people
- The first step is stakeholder identification - to identify everyone involved with or impacted by the project.
- For agile projects, the three essential roles are:
  o Team facilitator – a servant leader
  o Product owner – sets the product direction
  o Cross-functional team members – perform the work of the project
- When identifying stakeholders:
  o Over identify, rather than under identify those who are impacted
  o Consider the power and influence they will have on the project
  o Ask who else will be impacted and who else should I speak with about the project
- Pick the right project team
  o May not always be possible
  o Want to be there
  o Not just what they know, but who they know
- Project communication takes planning, and people involved in the project need frequent communication
  o Who needs information on the project
  o The level of detail they need
  o How frequently they need the information
  o How the information should be delivered
- Tools and templates:
  o Stakeholder Register
  o Communications Plan
  o Elevator Pitch
  o Project Deck
  o Status Report

- o Power-Interest Grid (see Chapter pro tip following this section)

Before she knew it, the day had come to an end. Siwan enjoyed the time with Harry. She realized how much she had learned about project management and felt better prepared to work with the people on his project. She looked forward to the second iteration with Harry.

Chapter Pro Tip: Over identify impacted people.

As Harry related, leaving a key stakeholder out of the plan may have consequences. Stakeholders that are affected may have an interest in or power over your project. If left out, they may not care, but some may have hurt feelings, or worse yet, want to cause harm to your project.

Project professionals often use what's called a Power-Interest Grid to determine how to manage stakeholders best. The Power-Interest Grid puts stakeholders into four quadrants based on their power and interest levels. The quadrant the stakeholder belongs to advises how to manage the stakeholder best:

Low power-low interest: Track these stakeholders to make sure you correctly identified their power-interest level. Watch as their status may change during the project.

Low power-high interest: Keep these stakeholders "in the loop." Ensure they receive the right messages, in the right format, at the right times for their group.

High power-low interest: Keep these stakeholders satisfied. Conduct periodic reviews or surveys to determine satisfaction levels. Ignoring a high power, low-interest individual may lead to unforeseen project issues. They may use their power and influence to attempt to address their dissatisfaction.

High power-high interest: Keep these stakeholders engaged. They need to be consulted, given tasks, and involved in some way in the project. They will be influencers who can have a significant impact on projects.

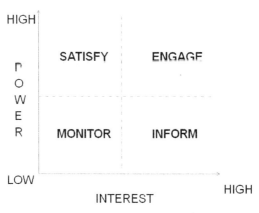

Figure 3: Power-Interest Grid

Agile Practice Guide reading: Chapter 4 provides more information about servant leadership and agile teams' composition.

PMBOK® Guide reading: Part I, Chapter 13, to learn more about stakeholder management.

Article: Got stake? (Holder) management in your project (Forman & Discenza, 2012)

Blog Article: Communicate, Communicate, Communicate (Frohnhoefer, 2020a)

Chapter Templates: Stakeholder Register, Communications Plan

2

ITERATION 2: DIG FOR REQUIREMENTS

The next morning when Siwan arrived at her office, she found a giant treasure map of what appeared to be Oak Island taped to her whiteboard. There was an "X" made with a marker and a dotted line connecting it to the words "Conference Room" written in a box on the whiteboard. Siwan grabbed her tea and laptop and headed to the conference room. She knew Harry would be waiting for her there.

After Harry quickly looked over the Stakeholder Register and Communications Plan Siwan worked on overnight, he nodded and then moved on to the next topic.

"R is for Requirements," started Harry. "Requirements aren't something you simply collect, or someone will hand to you – you need to dig for them like buried treasure. We call it 'elicitation' because we have to draw them out of stakeholders, just as you would have to dig buried treasure out of the ground."

"The first thing you need to do is plan your treasure hunt – a treasure map is worth a thousand words. Without the right requirements, you may not do the right project or deliver the products or services that meet your client's needs completely and correctly. Or you may end up taking more time and money than was budgeted. Even though agile projects may have changes made along the way, always starting in a meaningful direction is important."

Harry continued to explain the importance of requirements for products and services and looking at the problem from all angles, technical and non-technical. He used another metaphor to explain the importance of proper requirements. "I'm sure you've seen the movie Star Wars. What was the issue with the requirements for the Death Star?"

Siwan thought for a minute and realized that in the movie, the Death Star was virtually defenseless. "The Emperor focused so heavily on building a weapon of mass destruction that proper defenses were not considered - they were more of an after-thought," Siwan responded.

Harry nodded in agreement and said, "The rebel attack caused damage, but a single, well-targeted shot was able to destroy the entire project in an instant. All the expenses of building the project were realized, and the value was lost in seconds."

"Poor requirements elicitation and management constitutes the number two cause of project failure," continued Harry. "In one survey, 37% of companies reported poor requirements as the cause of project failure" (Larson, 2014).

"As the project manager for Movie Vault, you will be the one who develops the roadmap to discover the requirements. A business analyst has been assigned to your team to write the requirements once the project begins," Harry explained. "You will need to start by asking some key questions:

- What is the problem that needs to be solved?
- What information do we need?
- What information is already available from experts or historical resources?
- What are the sources for information that is not readily available and how can we get access to the sources?
- What is the best way to get the information?
- What is the best order for getting the information?
- How do we assure the reliability and credibility of the information?"

The team will have a business analyst, product owner, and Siwan collaborating to identify and document the requirements. It was further agreed that Siwan would facilitate and maintain the requirements plan. The business analyst and product owner would define the plan. Siwan would help them by documenting it.

Putting together the answers to these questions will lead them to understand and write the requirements. It will also help expose the needed information that they may not have thought of upfront.

The requirements team should compose a list of probing questions to help the team understand the product they need to build. Some people know they need something, but they cannot articulate clearly or at all what they need. Smart, to-the-point probing questions help trigger their thought process to provide the specific items' relevant information.

These questions need to consider technical and non-technical needs (for example, training and organizational relationships) while looking at all aspects of the organization as a framework. As the team embarks on their journey to gather information, they can start small and build on it through progressive elaboration. That is, a little initial information could provide clues for more information needs. Time should be set aside to determine the information required and then gather that information.

Eliciting requirements is like figuring out the "X" on a treasure map. Critical needs will point to where to dig for the next clue. Not every "X" will lead to treasure, but knowing where to search further helps define essential project requirements better.

Harry continued, "Now is a good time to review the Stakeholder Register, Siwan. The Stakeholder Register lists who has information and who knows where information is. Many subject matter experts, also known as SMEs, may contribute to understanding the project. Don't forget to factor additional time in for this important activity so that it is known ahead of time where you need to go for your information and insights."

For the last planning step, review the questions to determine if there should be a particular order to elicit the requirements information. Some of the ordering may be natural, such as getting high-level information before getting into details (for example, you can't build a house if the foundation isn't ready). Critical components, as defined by the sponsor, should be worked on first. The availability of key stakeholders may dictate the order in which questions are answered. Some of the ordering may simply be up to the team's discretion. It is crucial to think through how each session to obtain requirements will be structured.

"Once your plan is in place, you'll know better where to dig," said Harry. "At a minimum, you should plan to meet with:

- Dennis, the project sponsor,
- Jim, the Movie Vault product manager who is the client,

- other Movie Vault managers, and
- perhaps some of their end-users if Jim will arrange it.

And don't forget to ask each of them who else you should talk to."

Information Needed	Information Source	Method of Elicitation	Sequence
Movie Vault Requirements			
What are the expected roles using the application, and how many of each role will there be?	Jim at Movie Vault	Interview	1
What are the expected access requirements for each role?	Jim at Movie Vault Movie Vault Security Manager	Interview	3
What are the password rules expected to sign in?	Jim at Movie Vault Movie Vault Security Manager	Document review Interview	2
What administrative functions are needed?	Jim at Movie Vault Movie Vault Security Manager	Interview	4
What movie genres are supported?	Movie Vault Content Manager	Interview, Document review	6
What will users do to find movies?	Movie Vault Content Manager	Interview	5
What payment methods are used to purchase or rent movies?	Movie Vault Pricing Sheet	Document review	7
...	...	...	8
...	...	...	9

Figure 4: Sample Requirements Plan

"There are three essential techniques you will need to know to get the information: interviews, observation, and document reviews. You need to consider which is best for each piece of information and allocate time in your plan for these activities."

During interviews, a team member would meet with one or more people who have the information and ask them the questions to get the needed information to complete the project. Harry noted to be sure to run the meeting efficiently and effectively to make the best use of everyone's time.

Here's another acronym to remember to have **GREAT** meetings:

Guided – lead and facilitate the meeting; set and meet goals
Right People – have the right people to answer questions in the room
Effective – preplan the questions and be prepared to ask more
Agenda – send an agenda in advance; include key questions that might need preparation
Time-bound – respect the timeframe of the agenda; an hour meeting should last no more than an hour - schedule a follow-up meeting if required

Each session should enable the business analyst to collect information to write **SMART** requirements:

- Specific – Provide as much detail as possible:
  - What do I want to accomplish?
  - Why is this important?
  - Who is involved?
  - What resources are needed?
  - What constraints or limits must be considered?
  - Remember that for agile requirements, finding out more detail later is acceptable.
- Measurable – Performance of the requirement must be measurable. Be specific about "how much" and "how many."
- Achievable – Is it possible to implement the requirement?
- Relevant – Do we need this requirement? Should we do it?
- Time-oriented – Are there timing considerations for the requirements? By when or within what timeframe must the requirement complete?

Consider these two descriptions of the same requirement:

1. The Automated Teller Machine (ATM) will dispense cash

2. The ATM will dispense cash:
    a. To a validated and authenticated user with sufficient funds
        i. in the specified account
        ii. or in a linked account
        iii. or by overdraft protection
    b. Up to a maximum of $5,000 per day in $20 increments
    c. Within 2 minutes for the entire transaction

The second description satisfies the definition of SMART requirements. There are measurements and limits in place that can be validated and tested. If a two-minute limit is not achievable, new constraints can be set, or the project can be modified.

The business analyst gathering and documenting requirements should document any assumptions. For the ATM example, the analyst may have to consider additional information such as:

- How do we validate and authenticate users? Who are the users?
- What happens when the ATM runs out of cash or jams?
- Does the ATM need to provide a receipt?
- If we link an account or use overdraft protection, do we need to charge a fee?
- Is there a fee because this is a network user and not a client of our bank?
- Would clients prefer to select the denomination of bills or increments?

"There's never a guarantee that all the bases have been covered," Harry explained. "By being as specific as possible, the resulting product will have fewer gaps and issues, and the product development team will have greater clarity. They may still have to ask questions, but they can focus on lower-level details, rather than continue trying to figure out the bigger picture."

"I think I understand," Siwan mused. "We had a team that didn't get the right product developed since they never really understood what the client wanted. They asked lots of questions, but there were so many gaps that they got confused."

"Observation is another important way to gather information about how people will use a product or service," continued Harry. "Jim can help the team with questions about how the Movie Vault clients will use the application and may be able to set up meetings with some current clients. The answers may reveal more about the requirements needed. They will help the team better understand some non-technical issues such as user preferences and the level of training that may be required."

"Finally, you should also review existing documentation," stated Harry.

"What documents should we look at?" Siwan inquired.

"For documentation review, gather relevant, written documentation about the Movie Vault process that will use or integrate with the new software. Documents may include end-user documentation, past requirements, policies, and training manuals. You may find clues to requirements by reading through these documents," responded Harry.

After a brief pause, he continued, "Once you've reviewed the documentation, you may need to ask some follow-up questions that may have arisen during the documentation review."

Harry also suggested that it is essential for the business analyst to keep complete notes for all requirements gathering efforts. These should include who stated the need or where it was found, the level of importance, and any other details that could be helpful later.

Harry added, "At the end of each day of work on requirements, review your notes, and determine if the team needs more information. See if you can put questions into future sessions to get the information or schedule follow-up meetings or calls."

Elicitation will typically have three common issues which you need to plan to overcome:

1. *Availability of people to participate in interviews or observation.* Be flexible and schedule your discussions around the time availability of critical stakeholders. Also, consider if the information may be obtainable from someone else knowing and who is more available. For some information, it might be acceptable to ask for written answers to the interview questions. If time still cannot be scheduled, the project sponsor or client (in this case, Dennis and Jim) should be consulted.

2. *Conflicting information.* One stakeholder will likely say the product must be black, and another will say white. This disagreement is an important finding because it sheds light on where there may be inconsistencies in definitions, priorities, or the understanding of business practices. In this case, see what other people think. No matter what, you will have to sit down with these people and talk it through. Building a model or prototype may be helpful - they can see how it will appear. In an unresolved tie, a senior manager or the project sponsor may help with clarification or prioritization. An advantage of agile is that stakeholders will be able to see and experience project deliverables and have an opportunity to change them in the next release.

3. *Insufficient time.* A significant advantage of agile is "just in time requirements." All requirements do not have to be completed and approved before starting the project. The Agile

principle of accepting change will allow you to fill in details in the future. Remember also that "analysis paralysis" delivers no results – action is required. The best way to save time is to have a good plan and be sure each meeting is productive. Once again, the project sponsor should be able to help. In the worst case, just document where time ran out.

Requirements do not need to be perfect. Most importantly, they need to be testable or verifiable. This is especially true for an agile project where the focus is on getting smaller deliveries of usable products into the user's hands. There is time to explore alternatives and make changes based on user feedback. Getting comprehensive information comes at a high cost.

So how will the team know when they have all the information they need? Here are some of the signs – encountering more than one of these is usually a good sign that elicitation has gathered enough information to document the requirements:

- A good working solution is identified which can be documented (in the judgement of the customer).
- Stakeholders begin to provide redundant information.
- A successful working prototype or model is built.
- Stakeholders are slower to respond because they are unable to provide fresh information.
- The client or project sponsor tells you they are ready to approve what has been completed.

Harry continued, "Siwan, once elicitation completes, you should revisit the stakeholder register and communications plan to see if any updates are required. The business analyst will need to document the requirements. Unlike your cousin Rhett's project, which had a complete requirements document, agile projects'

REQUIREMENTS

1. SMART – not perfect
2. Techniques
   - Interview
   - Observation
   - Documentation review
3. Common Issues
   - Availability
   - Conflicting information
   - Inadequate time
4. Elicitation End
   - Working solution
   - Redundant information, slow response
   - Successfully built
   - Client or sponsor will approve

documentation is typically in user stories and epics. User stories are statements in the structure:

As a <u>role or user type</u>, I want to <u>take some action or achieve a goal</u>, so that <u>reason, value or benefit</u>."

"User stories written with this structure have three important aspects: card, conversation, and confirmation. These stories are recorded on index cards. The front of the card contains a title, the story, and the priority."

"Conversations about the user story will happen over time," Harry continued. "By the time the story is written, one will have already occurred. These conversations will be ongoing, especially when planning work or actively working on the requirement. The conversations take the place of writing highly detailed requirements."

"In contrast, the back or lower portion of the card will provide details, typically in bullet points, such as non-functional requirements, including limits, constraints, and acceptance criteria. These are the items that make the requirement SMART. The acceptance criteria specify the tests that will show the requirement has been met – these are the confirmations. The list of items on the back of the card may also grow over time as the conversations take place" (Jeffries, 2001).

41

As an example, a user story might be on the front of a card:

As a <u>Movie Vault client</u>, I want to <u>browse movies by genres</u> so <u>I can focus on the films I like to see</u>.

The back of the card may have some additional details as bullet points:

- Need to create a browse by genre page
- Clicking on a genre takes the user to a listing of movies categorized by this genre
- We need to tag all the movies with their genres (maybe more than one kind for a video)
- Genres in Movie Vault include:
    o Romance
    o Sci-Fi
    o Action – Adventure
    o Drama
    o Documentaries
- Acceptance criteria: all movies are tagged with one or more genres. All films belonging to the type are displayed when requested.

Epics are more meaningful stories that may need further break down into smaller stories that can fit into one iteration later. For example, on learning that there is a requirement for users to log on to the application securely, Jim, the product manager, may specify a need to log on. The epic might be:

As a <u>Movie Vault user</u>, I want to <u>securely log on to the site</u> to <u>access my purchased and rented movies</u>.

Some details to consider might be the acceptable formats of user names and passwords. As this is early in the development, this may be a sufficient requirement to get started. Later, as the team looks at the requirement more closely, there may be a need to break it down into smaller stories to cover additional actions such as:

- Registration of first-time users
- Two-factor authentication
- Ability to retrieve forgotten user names
- Ability to recover forgotten passwords
- Ability to reset expired passwords

TITLE: View by Genre	STORY PTS: 8	PRIORITY: M

As a: Movie Vault customer

I want to: view movie thumbnails by genre

So that: I can see the movies I may be interested in

Nonfunctional Requirements & Acceptance Criteria:

All movies are tagged with their genres (may be multiple), list TBD
Genre is page heading
Thumbnails and data will already be in database
Display thumbnails, titles, synopsis, major cast, price, and overall rating
Acceptance: Page renders within 5 seconds and content is compared to data.

Figure 5: Sample User Story

"Before we finish with requirements," Harry continued, "I want to emphasize the importance of collaboration for agile projects, especially when it comes to requirements. You will need to collaborate with Jim, the business analyst, and the stakeholders now on requirements, and throughout project execution to ensure the team produces the best product."

Collaboration requires a collection of skills. The best collaborators:

- are excellent communicators,
- know how to manage conflict appropriately,
- actively listen, and
- persuade others.

The best collaborative leaders:

- allow the team to participate in visioning for the team,
- encourage information sharing – no silos are allowed to form,
- understand that a diversity of thinking produces the best results,
- develop relationships with key people and encourage others to build relationships,
- know that collaboration is not about the technology used, but the people involved, and
- persuade the team to avoid harmful conflicts and increase productivity.

"I'm providing a Requirements Planning Template to use that will also help the planning process. I also have a Requirements Template that will aid documentation of user stories and epics," Harry wrapped it up. "Per the custom with many agile projects, Jim will work closely with the team to identify any new or missing requirements as the work continues. While he won't necessarily be able to work with the team every day, we will block out times when he will be available. He especially needs to be present for or represented in planning each iteration. He is what is known as the 'Voice of the Customer.'"

Siwan was thankful she didn't have a lot of work for the evening, yet she was ready to start jotting down some notes based on her requirements plan.

As with the previous iteration, Harry told a story to reinforce the key points. "Bad requirements lead to bad products, and bad products lead to business failure," he started. "Three years ago, my local bank put in new Automated Teller Machines (ATMs) that accepted new credit cards with chips. These cards had to stay inserted in the machine for the transaction, not just swiped initially. Whoever developed the requirements for the ATM forgot about human behavior."

"People were leaving their cards behind. Many were accustomed to grabbing the cash and driving away, assuming the transaction was complete. For several months, clients complained to the bank because they had to take someone else's card out of the machine before initiating their transaction. Fortunately, most people took the time to stop to return the cards to the bank manager."

"Within six months, the first version of the ATMs needed extensive modifications. The new software required users to remove the card before the machine would dispense the cash or receipts. This solution required both hardware and software changes. It was an expensive lesson for the vendor, but when they looked at the problem from all angles, they succeeded."

And once again, Harry summed up what they had covered during Iteration 2:

Chapter Summary

- R is for Requirements
- Requirements need a plan
  - Information needed
  - Where to find the knowledge or who has it
  - Best way to get the information and specifications and the order to get them in
- Three elicitation methods
  - Interviews
  - Observation
  - Document Reviews
- Three common elicitation problems
  - Availability
  - Inadequate Time
  - Conflicting Information
- Some ways to know when elicitation has enough information
  - An excellent working solution is identified or a prototype built
  - Stakeholders begin to provide redundant information or are slow to respond
  - The client or project sponsor tells you they are ready to approve the current requirements.
- After requirements elicitation, revisit the stakeholder register and communications plan to see if any updates are required
- User stories and epics document agile project requirements.
  - 3Cs: Card, Conversation, and Confirmations

ACROSTIC
ACRONYMS

PROJECT
Method

SMART
Requirements

GREAT
Meetings

- o Story or epic on the front of the index card
  - o Conversations to increase understanding of the requirement
  - o Epics are just stories which need a further breakdown to implement in a short time
  - o Confirmation and details of the requirement on the back
- Collaboration, which consists of a set of skills, is critical for eliciting and managing agile requirements throughout the project
- Tools and templates:
  - o Requirements Plan Template
  - o Requirements Template
  - o Elicitation Methods (see above)
  - o SMART – Specific, Measurable, Achievable, Relevant, Time-oriented
  - o GREAT Meetings – Guided, Right people, Effective, Agenda, Time-bound

Chapter Pro Tip: Interview the project sponsor and ask, "What does success look like to you?"

One great way to start elicitation is to meet with the project sponsor or client first and ask, "What does success look like to you?"

Getting the right requirements is not an easy task. Project management also involves making trade-offs in scope, time, budget, quality, and resources.

Sponsor responses to the open-ended question aid in understanding what the sponsor values. This understanding will inform future trade-offs and decisions. It is a valuable starting point for requirements – a high-level vision for the finished project and the expected benefits.

A common problem with projects is they produce a product or service that meets all requirements, but the benefits aren't realized. It is a must to understand the expected benefits to refine your needs.

Some other superior questions include:

- What are your biggest challenges and opportunities?
- What are some quick wins you'd like to achieve?
- What happens if we don't change or succeed?
- Who is impacted the most, and why?
- Who else will be affected?
- Who else should I speak with about the project?
- What else will impact the project?

Asking these open-ended questions can evoke valuable information to get the best user stories.

Agile Practice Guide reading: Unfortunately, neither the *PMBOK® Guide* nor the *Agile Practice Guide* meets their stated goal about describing the "how" of project management entirely. For more on user stories, see page 256 of *The Art of Agile Development* (Shore & Warden, 2008) and the book and articles below.

PMBOK® Guide reading: Part I, Section 5.2, to learn more about requirements overall. This section will refer you to another PMI publication that has more information about requirements elicitation and management.

Article: Requirements Management Made Easy (Davis & Zweig, 2000)

Article: User Stories and User Story Examples by Mike Cohn (Cohn, n.d.)

Book: Unearthing Business Requirements (Hossenlopp & Hass, 2008)

Chapter Templates: Requirements Planning, Requirements Document

CHAPTER 3

ITERATION 3: ORGANIZE OBJECTIVES

It was Wednesday, and Siwan was already feeling more confident that she could manage the project. When she arrived at the office, Harry was waiting for her in the conference room. On the whiteboard, he had written:

A man, a plan, a canal, Panama.

"Harry," Siwan started softly, "here at Xanadu, the programmers generally work up their plans and give the dates to the project manager. Is there something different we have to do?"

"Siwan, more than just a palindrome, the expression on the board tells a long story of a project that originally didn't have a good plan," Harry explained.

"After France succeeded with the construction of the Suez Canal, they were eager to repeat the project across Central America. Rather than do a complete plan, they did one or two site visits during the best weather times in 1881 and ordered digging to commence. Mudslides, snakes, poisonous spiders, yellow fever, and malaria claimed over 200 deaths per month. These issues were not a concern for the earlier project—the same heavy digging equipment used in the Suez Canal project rusted in the always damp jungle. The project failed and was abandoned for more than twenty years" (Panama Canal, 2018).

"Team involvement in planning is a good idea; repeating the past isn't planning. Dennis tells me many Xanadu projects run over time and budget. And while your project was a success, not all clients have been as delighted."

"Let's complete a plan for Movie Vault that you and your team can meet or exceed. I'm confident you can do it," said Harry supportively.

"Today, we're going to cover the real planning work you will have to do with your team for the project," Harry continued. "O is for Organize Objectives."

First, you should host a project kickoff meeting[4]. The meeting's purpose will be to introduce the team and key stakeholders to the project and its objectives. The roles and responsibilities of the team members will be explained. It is also an opportunity for the functional managers to learn how the resources they contribute to the project will be utilized. We'll work on planning the kickoff meeting when we talk about the team."

"The first part of your plan will include the activities to complete the requirements. Once the user stories are documented, you and the team will estimate all the known work. You must consider constraints and risks that may impact your estimates," Harry

---

[4] For smaller projects where the planning team is also the team doing the work, the kickoff meeting is usually held before planning. Large projects which may have separate planning and execution teams may either have two kickoff meetings or have one between the planning and execution processes of the project.

continued. "An example of a constraint is resource availability due to team vacations. A risk may be the uncertainty caused by a lack of experience with the required technology."

Much like a Work Breakdown Structure (WBS) for waterfall projects, agile projects use the product backlog[5]. The backlog contains the user stories and epics, an estimate for each, the priority, and an initial iteration in which they will be developed."

There are various ways in which the work may be prioritized. For example, each user story may just have a high, medium, or low priority. To help the team understand each story's importance, Harry told Siwan that Jim would use the MoSCoW method, which is also popular in business analysis (Agile, 2019). MoSCoW is an acronym for:

- **M**ust have – these stories must be included
- **S**hould have – these stories are of secondary importance
- **C**ould have – the team can decide if they want to do these – they are desirable but less important
- **W**on't have – these should be excluded (perhaps for now or always)

The estimation of agile projects is very different from traditional estimating. Rather than determine days or hours, agile estimation looks at factors such as complexity, difficulty, and risk, and compares each story relative to each other.

The simplest form of agile estimation is Tee Shirt Sizing. Each story is rated as XS (extra-small), S (small), M (medium), L (large), or XL (extra-large). XS is generally for minimal tasks, like

---

[5] The agile use of the word backlog does not have the same negative meaning as the normal English usage. Here, the backlog is simply a list of desired user stories and epics that are yet to be implemented. It is a "wish list," not a list of delayed features.

correcting a spelling mistake. XL means the story is an epic that should have a further breakdown into stories that can fit within one iteration. The team assigns the others after discussing the relative complexity, difficulty, and risk of each story.

A drawback for larger projects is that many stories fall into the same size category and are difficult to compare. Just as shirts made by different designers may have variations in size, ideas about the magnitudes of user stories will vary. (Cohn, 2013)

Another form of agile estimating that overcomes some of the shortcomings of t-shirt sizing is a game called Planning Poker. Poker Planning has more discussion and divides the stories up into more categories. These numeric categories are also referred to as story points. Story points will help determine how the work progresses and how many stories may be completed in an iteration.

With Planning Poker, each team member gets a deck of numbered cards. The numbers are usually Fibonacci[6] numbers:

$$0, 1, 2, 3, 5, 8, 13, 20, 40, 100, \text{ and } ? \text{ (unsure)}$$

The larger the number, the more complexity, difficulty, and risk. Correcting a simple typing mistake in some text might be 0. Developing a simple logon screen might be 1. Securely storing a password with secure, unbreakable encryption might be 8. An epic, which would need some further breakdown, is typically assigned 100. Other more significant numbers, such as 20 and

---

[6] Fibonacci numbers are a sequence of numbers where each number in the sequence is the sum of the previous two. Planning Poker does not need two 1s. Once the sequence gets higher, Planning Poker breaks the sequence to make it obvious that 40 is double 20 and 100 is 250% more than 40. The use of these numbers has been helpful in aiding teams to talk about the estimates without including whether one story is twice that of another (something that is difficult to measure or prove).

40, might be used for substantial features.

During planning poker, the person responsible for the requirements (in our case, Siwan) reads and describes a story. Each team member then selects a card to represent their estimate before everyone reveals their selections together. Those with high or low ratings have an opportunity to explain their choice, after which the participants estimate again. The game continues until a consensus occurs for each story or epic (Mountain Goat Software, 2020).

"Once story estimation is complete," Harry continued, "work starts on the product backlog. You and Jim will document the product backlog with the help of the team. Jim will have the primary responsibility for determining the order of work on stories based on his knowledge of the product and client priorities."

ID	Story Title	Story Points	Priority	Planned Sprint	Status
Administration Function					
1	Upload Movies	5	M	1	Completed
2	Update Movie Prices	2	M	2	In Progress
3	Correct Movie Data	2	M	2	In Progress
4	Replace Movie Thumbnail		W (for now)		Wont' Have
5					
6					
7					
8					
Customer Search Function					
9	Search by Genre	8	M	1	Completed
10	Search by Title	2	S	2	In Progress
11	Search by Reviews	13	C	3	Not Yet Started
12	Search by Cast Members	5	S	2	In Progress
13					
14					
15					
16					
Function / Feature #3					
17					
18					
19					

Figure 6: Sample Product Backlog

"The stories and epics will be placed into a series of iterations (short periods, generally around three weeks). Stories are grouped into useful functions. I'll provide you with a Product Backlog Template."

"Some iterations will complete incremental functionality for possible delivery to Movie Vault. In turn, Movie Vault can choose to make the software available to clients and request their feedback. The estimation and grouping will enable you to put together a prediction of approximate release dates, generally plus or minus 3-6 weeks, for Movie Vault."

"How will I know how many stories can be completed in an iteration?" Siwan asked.

"Great question, Siwan!" exclaimed Harry. "A good starting point is to assume that one product developer can complete one story point per day. If you have a 15-day (three weeks) iteration and a team of five, you should complete 75 story points in the first iteration. Another good rule of thumb is to have five to fifteen stories completed per iteration. The product developers will then decide among themselves who will work on each story" (Fuqua, 2015).

"While the product backlog will provide an initial list of iterations and deliveries, each iteration will require more careful planning. Jim will continue to guide the priorities and requirements updates. At the end of each iteration, you will consider the accomplishments, what adjustments to the work or team may be needed, and then plan the next iteration. This retrospective will let you determine if 75 is the right number of story points going forward."

"Quality for agile projects is often assumed to be a part of the product development; however, some integration testing is necessary before releasing software for clients. This testing helps

MILESTONE PLAN

A milestone plan contains:

- Major project activities
- Who performs and by when
- Listed in delivery date order

manage both quality and risk.

Jim will decide when software can be released for client use, monitor usage of releases, and bring more requirements, including bug fixes. At the start of each iteration, you will need to relook at the stories and see if there are any new requirements to include. This work will continue until Jim is satisfied with the product."

Harry continued, "Since all the hardware is in place and you are using only Xanadu programmers, you will not have to be concerned about a budget. Project managers, especially new project managers, rarely get to set their budget anyway. Plans for handling risks are also somewhat built into the agile methodology through the estimation, and an amount of uncertainty is acceptable. However, we will not need a separate risk analysis; that may not always be true for future projects. Now we can finalize all the plans and documentation needed to get the project underway."

In just a part of a day, it's not feasible to learn how to effectively create network diagrams and schedules using advanced software scheduling software. So, Harry suggested that Siwan should set up a Milestone Plan and present it to Dennis and the client (Andersen, 2006).

Agile projects often create a product roadmap – a diagram to illustrate the order in which the major features will be released. A milestone plan is an expanded roadmap that meets the team's needs and management. A milestone plan shows when the software's major components will be completed, along with the iterations.

The milestone plan will map out the initial work (e.g., project kickoff, requirements, product backlog development), the three-week iterations, the projected delivery dates with some time for testing, and the usual activities at the end of the project. Everything will need an estimate, a start date, and someone to be responsible. The team will plan everything with Siwan's facilitation. Harry supplied a Milestone Plan Template.

"Siwan, if you follow these basic principles, you will succeed," encouraged Harry.

Milestone/ Deliverable	Start Date	End Date	Responsible	Status	Comments
Project Kickoff Meeting	10/1/2020	10/1/2020	Siwan	COMPLETE	
Functional Requirements	10/2/2020	10/16/2020	Siwan	Not started	
Product Backlog Completed	10/19/2020	10/30/2020	Jim, Siwan, Team	Not started	
First Sprint	11/2/2020	11/20/2020	Jim, Siwan, Team	Not started	Each sprint begins with a review of the product backlog, has a daily stand up meeting, and ends with a retrospective and backlog refinement.
Second Sprint	11/23/2020	12/11/2020	Jim, Siwan, Team	Not started	Less time due to Thanksgiving holiday
Third Sprint	12/14/2020	1/8/2021	Jim, Siwan, Team	Not started	Extended a week due to winter holidays
...	...	...	...	...	...
Final Integration Testing	9/2/2021	9/15/2021	Siwan	Not started	
Final Demonstration and Turnover Meeting	10/1/2021	10/1/2021	Siwan	Not started	

Figure 7: Sample Milestone Plan

Siwan had absorbed a lot of information about planning and organizing the project and was more confident she would work with her team and succeed. Before departing for the day, Harry summed up what they had covered during Iteration 3:

Chapter Summary

- O is for Organize Objectives
- Planning should start with a kickoff meeting to introduce the team and the project
- Planning is an essential team activity
  - First, identify all the known work, create the user stories, and an estimate for each story
  - Rather than estimate time, agile estimation compares the relative complexity, difficulty, and uncertainty (risk) of each story
  - Organize the stories and epics into iterations, called the product backlog
  - The product backlog replaces the WBS of predictive projects
  - Use the information to determine when the product components are releasable to the client
- Before releasing any part of the project for client use, it is essential to test to ensure quality and reduce failure.
- Document the milestone plan and get client and management buy-in
  - Major project activities
  - Iterations
  - Deliveries in ascending date order
- In the PROJECT methodology, a milestone plan is an expanded product roadmap, often used by agile projects to indicate the sequence of feature development
- The milestone plan meets the needs of both the team and management
- Tools and templates
  - Product Backlog Template
  - Milestone Plan Template
  - Tee Shirt Sizing
  - Estimation Poker

Knowledge Nuggets

Despite decades of research and improvement, project failure rates are still too high. By some accounts and surveys, up to 20% of projects even fail outright. Double-digit percentages of projects experience challenges in one or more ways. Improper selection of the life cycle hurts these statistics.

Agile projects differ from waterfall projects in several significant ways:

- Estimation compares complexity, difficulty, and uncertainty or risk between tasks (user stories).
- In place of complete, early planning, agile projects start with a product backlog. The backlog is divided into iterations. New and changed requirements are acceptable at the start of each iteration. Some agile methods refer to these as "sprints"; yet, for now, we will use a more generic term: iterations.
- Each iteration can re-think estimates and requirements, so the product backlog is fluid.
- This approach means deliveries will continue to move out later in the project.
- Product developers will always believe that testing is built into the iterations. The reality is that any product needs to have thorough and independent testing.

Agile methods are often inappropriate for projects with fixed deadlines or budgets. They are best when a large amount of uncertainty, especially in scope, is acceptable. It is more valuable to begin the project than spend time

61

> finalizing scope. R&D, exploratory, or other projects in need of client feedback often benefit from agile methods.

Agile Practice Guide reading: Section 5.2.2 contains more information about backlog planning.

PMBOK® Guide reading: Part I, Section 5.4, to learn more about the WBS. Chapter 6 on creating schedules is a little more advanced, so you might want to revisit it in the future—section 6.4 covers estimation. Chapter 11 covers risk management.

Articles:
Estimating with T-Shirt Sizes (Cohn, 2013)

Planning Poker (Mountain Goat Software, 2020)

Milestone Planning—A Different Planning Approach (Andersen, 2006)

Books:
Risk Assessment Framework: Successfully Navigating Uncertainty (Frohnhoefer, 2019b)

Chapter Templates: Product Backlog, Milestone Plan

CHAPTER 4

ITERATION 4: JELL WITH THE TEAM

Regardless of the project methodology, the importance of teamwork is constant. On the beginning of the fourth day, when Siwan arrived at the office, she found another message on her whiteboard:

Together
Everyone
Achieves
More

And underneath it was written:

Breakfast? Meet me at the coffee shop on the corner.

Siwan knew today was going to be about teamwork but wondered about the new meeting venue as she hurried out the door and down the block. As usual, Harry was waiting, this time with a hot breakfast sandwich on a bagel and her favorite tea.

This little reward for Siwan's constant learning was his way of reinforcing the lesson before it started.

"Good morning, Siwan," Harry began. "Remember, during our first day together that I mentioned people make or break projects? The team is one essential group, and you are going to have to be able to work with them quickly and effectively."

Harry continued, "As we discussed, you will be the team facilitator and project manager. Movie Vault will provide a product owner. There will be cross-functional team members in the roles of business analyst, developers, and testers."

"Communications and teamwork are critical to every project. We're going to start building your awareness of teamwork today. I will provide you with some additional skills during the next few iterations."

"J is for Jell with the team," Harry continued. "The project manager and the team need to work closely together to achieve the desired results."

Harry went on to give an example of failed teamwork. During the 1970s, he and Heda worked on a project to produce a sophisticated supercomputer. The hardware and software were developed in parallel to speed up the work. Unfortunately, there wasn't a lot of communication between the two teams.

When the first integration test was conducted, it was found that the hardware design had the bits numbered from right-to-left, and the software team had numbered them from left-to-right. This disparity caused an enormous amount of rework and significantly delayed the project. When combined with other factors, the project was postponed sufficiently for a competitor to beat them to the sales. The project failed, and this led to the overall failure of the company.

"You've probably heard," Harry continued, "that teams go through development stages – forming, storming, norming, performing, and closing. With the edge of getting to influence who is on your team and your development as a project manager and team leader, we're all hoping the 'storming' part is minimal. Excellent teamwork and your management of the team will be essential."

Trust is what makes teams work well. As Harry had instructed during the first iteration, Siwan had to learn to give trust first to be trusted. By leading by example and being in a position of servant leadership, Siwan would build an environment of trust quickly. It would initially be fragile, but she could take steps to ensure the team worked well together over time.

Servant leadership is a form of leadership where the leaders serve the team before meeting their own needs. Acting as a mentor and coach, the leader has a responsibility to:

- remove roadblocks and help every team member achieve their goals,
- involve team members in decision making as much as possible, and
- build a sense of community and team identity.

The servant-leader tends to build stronger relationships and more trust with the team (Mindtools).

Confidence is a critical ingredient in leading effectively. To improve your self-confidence, make a list of your strengths that helped you achieve your past accomplishments and how these can lead you to future success. Next thing you should ask yourself– "Why should people follow me? Think of the situations when you led yourself through tough challenges.

Agile teams are usually cross-functional, as we learned during the first iteration. For this project, the business analyst, developers, and testers were all from different departments. Siwan will also need to be acquainted with the functional managers to whom they will also report.

"Siwan, you will need to spend some time at the start of the project getting to know the team and their managers more personally. Some of them you may know and have worked with, some will be people with whom you are not acquainted."

Siwan will have to work with the team to build trust, and everyone on the team will need to get to know each other better. Harry suggested one way to encourage the process would be to do some icebreaking and team-building exercises at the start of all critical team meetings or other appropriate times.

"One exercise I found to be very effective is to ask the team to write about their 'dream trip'," explained Harry. "Ask them to imagine the project is over, and as a reward for a job well done, that they are given one month with an unlimited budget to take a trip to anywhere in the world. They can choose anyone they want to accompany them. Give them ten to fifteen minutes to write out their itinerary – ask them to be specific and as detailed as possible about

DREAM TRIP EXERCISE

Team members write and share a detailed itinerary and plans for an all-expenses paid trip to the location of their choice.

- where they are going
- how they are going to get there
- who is accompanying them
- where they will stay, and
- what they will do ("The Team Building Directory - Dream Trip," 2018).

TRUST

> Research has shown that teams need trust to perform well and to become high performing.
>
> Be sure to give trust to gain trust.

"When time is up, everyone takes turns sharing their trips for five minutes. In under an hour of interaction, much about the style, preferences, and personality of each team member surfaces."

Harry also suggested that Siwan schedule monthly team lunches and other fun events so everyone would get to know each other better. He asked Siwan to do an Internet search for additional team-building exercises – that would be her homework for the evening.

Another attribute of agile teams is that they usually are co-located to facilitate collaboration. Harry continued, "I've already spoken with Dennis, and we are going to do our best to make sure the team has working space together. The product owner from Movie Vault may not be there daily. However, we made it clear to Jim that a regular presence, particularly at the start and end of development iterations, is essential. Being co-located will also help you in building rapport with the team."

Harry next wanted to talk about management through influence. While it is a critical skill that managers of all levels need to master, it's especially crucial for project managers. They do not have any direct management authority over the project team.

"At Xanadu, we communicate with WhatsApp and Slack," stated Siwan. "I can let the team know when we are going to get together."

"I'm not familiar with those applications," said Harry. "Maybe you could show me how they work?"

As they finished breakfast, Siwan gave Harry a quick overview of the applications and promised to share more detail later.

Harry explained that Siwan had to acknowledge the team's work as a group and as individuals (Umlas, 2006). Things to recognize could include:

- Recognition when key milestones are met, even with just a "thank you."
- When someone accomplishes something extraordinary, report it to management in the next status report, being sure to credit those who made an effort.
- Anyone who did something extraordinary more than twice in a quarter should be nominated for a quarterly Xanadu management award. The award is a $100 gift certificate for the employee and a guest to have dinner at a delicious San Diego restaurant.

The scheduled monthly team lunches or other fun events would represent opportunities to provide more public recognition.

Showing Siwan by example, she was learning and absorbing the information she needed. As the morning turned to noon, Harry led Siwan down the block further to a small café. Here they enjoyed a light lunch as they continued their conversation. By the time they moved back to the Xanadu conference room, they were ready for the next topic.

Suddenly, Harry's cell phone rang in his pocket, and he pulled it out to answer. Siwan was completely surprised as his phone had been silent up until now. He listened carefully for a few minutes, occasionally nodding his head. When finished, he thanked the caller, then hung up.

"Siwan," Harry began, looking more concerned than ever, "there's been a slight complication with your project. Dennis met with the Xanadu resource manager The in-house QA team will be engaged in other projects when we expect them to work on the Movie Vault application. He's gotten senior management to sign-off on a contract with Pointeast Technologies, a leading IT service company in Manilla."

"Pointeast has a rigorous independent software testing service and an excellent reputation," Harry stated confidently. "As a result, you will not just have to work with the development team in San Diego; you will also have a virtual team in the Philippines. We'll need to spend some time this afternoon preparing to handle a virtual team. We can make this work using Zoom video conferencing and other tools so the developers and testers can collaborate as needed together."

Harry explained that while all communications will be in English, English will be a second language for most of the team. In addition to the points already discussed, Siwan will have to communicate clearly and concisely to be understood. She will also have to make sure her messages were received and interpreted as intended. She has to practice active listening, confirming what she hears in her conversations with them.

While much of the communications may be conducted by email, Siwan will also have to maintain personal contact with the Pointeast project manager and team. Harry recommended the use of Zoom conferencing so that she can have face-to-face discussions. The use of conferencing applications will enable them to obtain clarity and closure more quickly. They can also participate in some meetings with the rest of the team.

"Time will present some issues," Harry stated. "First, daylight savings time is not observed in the Philippines. The country is fifteen hours ahead of San Diego when daylight savings time is observed in California, sixteen hours when it is not. So optimal time for conference calls will tend to be around the end of the workday in San Diego. This time will be the start of the next workday in the Philippines. Siwan, you will have to take this into account when scheduling meetings and planning deadlines."

Finally, the distance itself will present challenges, such as making it more challenging to build trust, feeling isolated, lacking social interaction, and failing to instill an overall team spirit. Siwan will have to research other cultural differences such as holidays to celebrate and factor them into plans (Bailey, 2013). Harry supplied her with a Virtual Team Contact Template to record critical information about different cultural needs.

Team Member	Role	Location (Time Zone)	Hours +/-	Work Hours or Shift	Preferred Communication Methods and Contact	Comments
Siwan	PM	San Diego (Pacific)	0		Email: Siwan@xanadu.com	
Dennis	Manager	San Diego (Pacific)	0		Mobile: +1.619.555.1212	
Richard	Business Analyst	Kihei, HI (HAST)	-3		Mobile: +1.808.555.1212 Email: RickHI@xanadu.com	No prior virtual team experience / relocating to San Diego during the project
Rosamie	Pointeast Manager	Manila (PHT)	+15		Zoom Meeting: https://Zoom.US/123456 Contact by whatsapp first: RosamiePE	Prefers f2f video conferencing

Figure 8: Sample Virtual Team Contract List

Harry advised that if they had reasonable requirements, Siwan could start working with the QA team early. Plans could be put in place that would have a high probability of success. Harry was confident that Siwan would be able to handle this new aspect of the project.

"We have one last topic today that we need to discuss," continued Harry, "and it's an important one. As we discussed earlier, a big event for the team will be the project kickoff meeting, and you will need to plan for it carefully. The meeting will be a chance for Jim, from Movie Vault, to meet the team as the client, and Dennis will be the Xanadu project sponsor."

"Who else should be invited?" Siwan inquired.

"Since some of the team members report to different functional managers, the functional managers should be invited as well. They can hear how their resources will be used and what they can do to support the project."

Figure 9: Sample Kickoff Meeting Agenda

"The team will begin to get acquainted. Together, the team members will learn the client and project sponsor's vision for high-level scope and approach. If timed right, the project manager from Pointeast could also join via video conference. This way, the team understands there will be remote participation in the not too distant future."

"You should think about the agenda for this meeting – I've got a Kickoff Agenda Template you may consider. You may also want to be sure it is a GREAT meeting, as we discussed when looking at meetings for eliciting requirements. Having a GREAT meeting will ensure everyone is well-prepared for the meeting and will be able to immediately contribute."

Take Your Meetings from Good to GREAT!

It is estimated that project managers spend up to 50% of their time in meetings. Commit to having GREAT meetings.

Figure 10: GREAT Meetings

Harry explained the kickoff meeting is where Siwan should share:

- the high-level product information,
- a draft milestone plan, and
- the basics of how the team will work in the new, agile project environment.

The work of creating the product backlog should begin the day after the kickoff meeting, if possible. Setting expectations up front will help manage the subsequent deliveries.

Clarity of the purpose, plan, and primary responsibilities will get the team on the right path, and Siwan will be in place leading them. They can build on the momentum and excitement set in motion by the kickoff meeting. The clarity and energy mean that the team will spend minimal time in the "storming" phase.

As the day and iteration ended, Harry started another story. "Around fifteen years ago, someone I mentored just like you had a difficult project. His goal was to test, upgrade, and retest 10,000 computer systems."

"He hired a team of ten temporary workers to design and perform the tests. The client signed off on the test plans, and the project moved forward. The team was doing well when the client suddenly demanded a new change. The timeline for the project was going to be cut by three to four months. A new, end-of-year deadline was set in place of the prior deadline of the following spring."

Harry continued to explain that while the team continued testing, the project manager worked out a plan to complete the work on time and deliver the client's systems. He shared it with the team to get their buy-in. It would require the team to expand to thirty to accommodate all the work. Because the team worked so well together, they were able to help the project manager bring the new team members up to speed.

The team split into three groups of ten: one to do the upgrades, one to test, and the third to do a final inspection, packing, and shipping. One of the original team members took charge of each of the new teams and reported daily to the project manager. If upgrades or testing were falling behind, some packing and shipping team members were diverted to help. The systems were all delivered, and the client signed off on the work – the project was a massive success because of teamwork.

Harry, as usual, summarized their learning for the iteration:

Chapter Summary

- J is for Jell with the team
- The agile team members include a facilitator, product owner, and cross-functional team members that perform the work of the project
- The facilitator is a servant leader – mentoring and coaching instead of leading and directing:
  - Removes roadblocks
  - Involves the team in decision-making
  - Builds the team identity
- Leaders need confidence – why should people follow you?
- Teamwork is critical for success
  - Trust is essential to healthy teams
  - Teambuilding activities help the team to jell and develop trust
- Team involvement in decision-making increases buy-in to plans and decisions
- Agile teams usually are co-located to increase collaboration and teambuilding
- Management by influence, not authority
  - Trust and teambuilding build influence
  - The project team needs to participate in decision making
  - Acknowledge the work of the team
- Cultural challenges of virtual teams
  - Time: time zones and perceptions of time
  - Language and communications
  - Distance
- Project kickoff meeting
  - Invite the sponsor, client, project team, and functional managers

- o   Have a GREAT meeting
- o   Include virtual teams
- Tools and templates
  - o   Virtual Team Contact Template
  - o   Kickoff Meeting Agenda Template
  - o   Dream Trip Exercise
  - o   Servant Leadership
  - o   Acknowledgment
  - o   GREAT Meetings

Even with the addition of the virtual QA team, Siwan remained confident that she could handle the teamwork required. She went home to eat dinner before starting her homework.

Knowledge Nuggets

<table>
<tr><td>Chapter Pro Tip: Know the team and who they know.</td></tr>
</table>

First and foremost, get to know your team very well. In addition to team-building exercises, schedule one-on-one meetings. Consider questions such as:

- Where do you see yourself in five years?
- What knowledge or skills do you think you need to develop to get there?
- Within the scope of our work, what kind of assignments do you believe would help?
- What items should the team work on together?
- What can I do to support your development?

Questions like these will not just help you get to know your team better – your team will see you as a leader that is there to support their success.

In a much less direct way, get to know who the team knows, both inside and outside your organization. Teams with challenging assignments don't always have all the answers. When questions and challenges arise, help your team think about who they might know who could help them find a solution.

Agile Practice Guide reading: Section 4.3 is about Team Composition. Chapter 6 discusses Organizational Considerations for Project Agility (section 6.5 focuses on MultiTeam Coordination and Dependencies).

PMBOK® Guide reading: Part I, Chapter 9, to learn more about project resource management.

Article: How Different Cultures Understand Time (Lewis, 2014)

Book: The Power of Acknowledgement (Umlas, 2006)

Website: http://www.ventureteambuilding.co.uk/team-building-activities/ provides a list of more than 60 team building activities and exercises

Chapter Templates: Virtual Team Contact, Kickoff Meeting Agenda

CHAPTER 5

ITERATION 5: EXECUTE EFFORTLESSLY

On Friday morning, Harry was waiting in Siwan's office for her arrival. On the whiteboard, she saw:

Soft skills will be the **FAD** during execution:

- **F**eedback and **F**ollow Up
- **A**ccountability
- **D**elegation

"Did you finish your homework?" Harry inquired.

"I did," Siwan replied enthusiastically. "I have a copy for your review."

Harry took the time to review Siwan's teambuilding exercises and gave her some feedback before starting project execution.

"E is for Execute. We've talked a lot about planning," Harry began. "If you have the best possible plan in place, execution will take far less effort. New problems with people will emerge, and you will need to be prepared to handle them. While the team works on the project, your challenges will shift from planning to making things happen. But you need to trust them and let the team do the work."

Harry continued his explanation, "One year, a project management class I was teaching at a university had a team of web developers in attendance. They always seemed very down, so one day I asked them what was happening. While they were well paid, their manager made all the decisions and managed their workday to the hour."

"They had no room for creativity, innovation, or even to make simple suggestions. They were completely micromanaged. There was a total absence of trust; their manager thought he knew better than everyone. Three months later, they all quit, and the company had to close."

"We already discussed the importance of collaboration for requirements during the second iteration," Harry continued. "Collaboration is vital to continue to manage requirements throughout project execution since new requirements may be introduced between iterations. You, Jim, the team, and other stakeholders will need to continue to work collaboratively."

EXECUTION

After having a good plan, soft skills help agile project managers achieve the best performance:

- Feedback and
- Follow up
- Accountability
- Delegation

"Agile projects also require a lot of feedback and follow up. Agile events are practices that require collaboration and provide much of the necessary input and follow up."

With agile projects, execution is performed in short intervals, typically three weeks in length. Some agile methods refer to these iterations as sprints. Each sprint includes four important events (formerly called ceremonies) that keep the project progress on track. One takes place daily, and the others take place at the end of each sprint.

These events are:

- **Daily stand-up meeting:** Every day, the full team (facilitator, product owner, cross-functional team members) meets for around 15-20 minutes to review progress – an opportunity for feedback and follow up. The time is limited to answer essential questions and make commitments for the next day. All other discussions take place outside this meeting. The questions are:
  - What did I achieve yesterday?
  - What do I hope to achieve today?
  - What may prevent me from achieving this goal?

Each team member answers in turn, and the meeting ends after everyone presents and makes new commitments.

- **Retrospective:** Like lessons learned (usually associated with project closing), retrospectives are held at the

AGILE EVENTS

- Daily stand-up – Progress (follow up), commitment, and feedback (on roadblocks)
- Retrospective – Continuous improvement
- Demonstration – Visual demonstration of progress
- Backlog Refinement – Mark off completed work, add new requirements, plan the next sprint

81

end of each iteration. They are not about placing blame for sprint failures but focus on future changes. Retrospectives provide an opportunity for continuous improvement throughout the project. (Harry also provided a template for recording the retrospectives.)

Key questions to discuss are:
- o What should we start doing in the next sprint to improve?
- o What didn't work well, and should stop doing it?
- o What worked well in the last sprint and should be continued?

- **Demonstration:** At the end of each sprint, demonstrate the work products for the product owner, client, and other key stakeholders. The product owner can accept, reject, or request changes to the work completed.

- **Backlog refinement:** At the end of every sprint, maintain the backlog and plan the next sprint. Completed stories are marked as complete. Any requested changes or bug fixes are added as new user stories. The facilitator and product owner work with the team to review priorities and determine what user stories to complete in the next sprint.

While the team will self-organize to work on the next sprint, many more pieces of work would likely reveal themselves during execution. These will include bug fixes, overlooked requirements, and feedback from the product owner, Jim, among other things. Siwan had to learn to delegate to team members, rather than try to do it all herself.

During project execution, Siwan needs to follow-up on her follow-ups and meet regularly with every team member individually. Once again, this may depend on experience level.

START
Using Planning Poker
Developing common user interfaces that can be re-used. The user experience is better if we have one date-picking tool, rather than a lot of different ones.
Spending more time in testing – it will reduce bugs to fix in future sprints.

STOP
Using tee shirt sizing – it is not as useful as Planning Poker for estimating stories.
Stop checking email so frequently – limit to 3x per day.

CONTINUE
Looking for reusable code – it is more efficient and helps us finish our sprints.
Thanks, Swran, for motivating us!

Figure 11: Sample Retrospective

"The best manager I ever worked with was Nathan," stated Harry, "He walked by everyone's office or cubicle at least once a day to greet them by name. He'd say, 'Hi Harry, how are you today? Is everything on track?' If I responded, I was fine, Nathan would move on to the next office. If I had an issue, he'd sit down and ask me to explain how I was thinking of solving it. Usually, these just ended with comments like 'You're on the right track, Harry,' and he'd move to the next office."

Follow-up is also crucial for any tasks that remain uncompleted just before the end of an iteration, especially if multiple team members share the responsibility. It's a typical team mistake to think that handoffs of work are happening as planned – someone may be out sick or delayed in finishing their work. Still, the rest of the team may not know it or think about it. These types of hidden, unfounded assumptions can make otherwise successful projects fail.

Follow-up is required to make sure the most important and critical activities are being completed as planned. If they are not, corrective action may be necessary. Be sure that roadblocks raised in daily stand-up meetings are addressed promptly. In some instances, it may be prudent to verify status updates to ensure that completed work meets the required standards.

"Feedback is also critical to execution success," continued Harry. "As a project manager, you will need to give both praise and constructive criticism. It is best to remain professional in both cases; be direct, and stay with the facts. Focus on the desired outcomes, give feedback often, and be as specific as possible."

"Also, try to emphasize the positive aspects. You may be tempted to say, 'you never contribute enough ideas to the team.' Instead, say, 'I reviewed the meeting minutes, and you haven't contributed any new ideas during our discussions of innovation. What are your thoughts on what the team should be doing?' This question will open up a two-way dialog and get to the root cause of any issues faster. It focuses on leading the team member to find a solution rather than just offering criticism."

As Harry pointed out on the first day, people need their leader to acknowledge their excellent work and positive contributions. There needs to be a balance between praise and criticism, emphasizing the team's appreciation. Leaders who only comment on performance when there are issues or problems will quickly lose the team's trust. And trust is essential for a leader to be able to lead by influence.

"Perhaps the most important thing you will need to do during project execution is to hold people accountable," Harry explained.

"Team members are expected to perform their job responsibly, make and meet commitments, and take responsibility to deliver. To emphasize this responsibility, you ask them to participate in daily stand-up meetings, contribute to the product backlog, and provide estimates. They choose the schedule, and you are negotiating with them, representing what is needed for the project. Many project managers make the mistake of dictating the schedule. Once the team buys into the schedule, the project manager ensures that the schedule and interdependencies between the cross-functional team members are met on time."

Harry went to the whiteboard and began to write again:

The 4Cs:

1. Clarity
2. Commitment
3. Comment
4. Coaching

"It looks like these are necessary to hold people accountable. Is that true?" Siwan inquired.

"That's right. Being clear about what is needed and following up on commitments made are the first two of four steps in holding people accountable," answered Harry. "When goals aren't being met, and activities aren't completed as planned, the team members need to know. They need quality feedback – the third step."

"The fourth step is coaching and mentoring. You will need to have discussions with those not performing up to expectations. They must understand what is expected and the consequences for the team and organization if the expectations are not met."

"This is not a form of criticism, but an opportunity to discuss with the team member why they haven't been able to meet their commitments. You will find out about the support and resources they may need to get back on track."

"Siwan, yesterday I mentioned my mentee, who was responsible for the project testing 10,000 computer systems. Once that project moved into execution, and the testing and upgrade of the equipment started, delegation, follow-up, feedback, and accountability were key to getting the team to their revised end-of-year goal. Every day ended with a brief meeting between the project manager and the team leads to review issues. The project manager made sure that requests for additional resources and tools were quickly reviewed and necessary actions were taken. The team truly became a high performing team."

"I'm confident I can build a high performing team," stated Siwan, "thanks to your guidance, Harry."

Harry knew that Siwan would face many challenges, especially with the addition of a virtual QA team located in another country. She would not have time to do any architecture, coding, or testing on this project – she had to keep her eye on all the moving parts to ensure the team was performing.

Harry explained, "Unfortunately, new project managers often lack confidence or fear loss of control, leading to lower levels of delegation. Unfortunately, loss of control happens typically when project managers fail to delegate and do too much by themselves. They have to resist the 'I can do it better or faster myself' thinking and set up a successful delegation."

Delegation taps into the power of the team to accomplish project activities. It can be a learning experience, boost team confidence, and be a step toward developing a high performing team when done correctly. Siwan will achieve more by delegating what others can do, even if they are not up to her competence level. Delegation allows her to focus on planning and other responsibilities.

There are four critical elements to successful delegation:

1. Select the right person for the task and empower them to get it done.
2. Clearly communicate any requirements and expectations.
3. Discuss the "what" but leave the "how" to the team member.
4. Demonstrate confidence the team member will complete the assignment

"Based on the level of experience of the team member," Harry pointed out, "you can adjust your expectations. A junior team member with little or no experience with a task should formulate a plan of action to accomplish the task, then come back to you for approval. Someone very senior may complete the task and report back when it is done."

Also, do not just communicate – explain. Be sure the expectations are clear. Explain what is or is not acceptable in the finished work. Ask questions to be sure your delegation is understood.

Harry continued, "Siwan, I know you will be able to reach that goal - you've been doing well in absorbing the material. We won't work together over the weekend, so please take some time to reflect on what you've learned. If you have any areas where you want more information, dig into the additional materials I've provided. We'll meet on Monday and Tuesday, and your work on the Movie Vault project will begin on Wednesday."

Harry wrapped up the iteration with a summary:

Chapter Summary

- E is for Execute
- Proper planning makes execution progress more smoothly
- Collaboration for requirements between the project manager, product owner, the team, and other stakeholders is critical
- Soft skills are the FAD for execution:
  o Feedback and Follow Up
  o Accountability
  o Delegation
- Work will happen in iterations or sprints – three-week intervals
  o Team and product owner decide on stories and epics to work on
  o Team self-organizes to choose who performs each task
  o At the end of the iteration, progress is evaluated, and completed work is groomed or removed from the product backlog
- Four important agile project events
  o Daily stand-up meeting to determine progress
  o Retrospectives to learn how to improve the next spring
  o Demonstration to allow the product owner and client to review work
  o Product backlog refinement to discuss priorities and add new stories for new requirements and bug fixes
- Give Frequent Feedback
  o A mix of praise and constructive feedback
  o Keep it professional

- - Emphasize the positive
  - Focus on solutions, not the criticism
- Follow up early and often
  - Meet/touch base with team members
  - Urgent tasks need more follow up
  - Don't make hidden or unfounded assumptions
- Hold people accountable
  - 4Cs – clarity, commitment, comment, coach
  - Be clear what's needed
  - Follow-up on tasks and delegations needs to be early and often
  - Give frequent feedback – praise and criticism
  - Coach and mentor to sustain and improve performance
- Delegation is important
  - Select and empower the right person for the job
  - Communicate "what" – let the team member work on "how"
  - Demonstrate confidence that the task can be performed to expectations
  - Make adjustments for the level of experience of the team member
- Tools and templates
  - Retrospective Template
  - Agile Events
  - Delegation
  - Feedback
  - Follow Up
  - Accountability

Siwan left feeling confident about what she would be able to accomplish with Harry's help. She would spend some time studying over the weekend to prepare for the project to start on Wednesday.

Chapter Pro Tip: Say "no" without saying "no," set limits without setting limits.

The best project managers learn to say "no" without actually using the word "no." "No" has an air of finality and disempowers the team. It is also a good idea to avoid phrases like "Yes, but ..."

Try some of these alternatives instead:

- Yes, and in exchange, I will need "x." Will that work? (say yes and get something in return)
- I'm worried about "x" now, so would "y" and "z" work instead? (suggest alternatives)
- Given "x," how would you like me to proceed? (point out a downside to "yes" and get input)
- Would you please help me prioritize these actions? (support the priority of a "yes" to be considered)
- May I make an alternative suggestion? (a more direct way to suggest alternatives)

Similarly, setting arbitrary limits can be equally challenging. Rather than set a limit on the number of issues, for example, find another approach. For example:

- Define multiple categories for issues and clearly define what goes in each "bucket"
- Specify time frames for addressing items in each category
- When there are more issues than you can handle, you can either wait it out or bring in more resources
- If a higher number of issues than expected happens for a prolonged period, you can re-think quality plans and re-define priorities

> Using these techniques will empower the team and establish you as a respected and trusted leader.

Agile Practice Guide reading: Section 5.2 offers information about agile events (formerly known as ceremonies).

PMBOK® Guide reading: The PMBOK mentions many skills but does not provide much information about them. Section I, Chapter 4, on project integration management, covers some aspects of expertise.

Articles:
Project Manager Accountability (Jordan, 2017)

What are Agile Ceremonies? (Carpenter, 2018)

Website: Learn more and test your delegation skills at Mindtools.com ("How Well Do You Delegate? Discover Ways to Achieve More", 2018)

Chapter Template: Retrospective

CHAPTER 6

ITERATION 6: CONTROL CASUALLY

On Monday morning, Siwan arrived early, refreshed from the weekend, and feeling confident from her review and study. Harry was already waiting for her, and once they exchanged pleasantries about their weekends, he was ready to begin.

"C is for control," Harry started. "With controlling, you set your project parameters, monitor them as the project is in progress, and make some changes as necessary. Controlling is only second in importance to planning. One common mistake that new project managers make is either to under control or over control. Think of under-steering or over-steering a car – neither is likely to get you to your destination safely."

"So, what is the right amount of control?" Siwan inquired.

"The right amount of control is in place when there are no surprises," Harry exclaimed. "A firm and steady guiding hand – disciplined but with a suitable level of informality. Pay more attention to overall trends than one-time small deviations. And have checks and balances in place for your most important constraints such as time and resources. We'll consider how to accomplish the right level of control best today. Do you remember the construction of Petco Park, the baseball stadium in San Diego?"

Siwan nodded – she went to ball games regularly with her cousin. She knew there were some problems before the stadium opened.

"When the construction was about half completed, the entire budget had been spent. How can something like this happen?" Harry asked.

"I see," Siwan mused, "there must have been some inadequate controls in place. Otherwise, how could they miss a gap that big?"

"Precisely!" exclaimed Harry. "Without appropriate controls, projects aren't completed as planned, and clients are usually unhappy. Let's take a look at the basics to put in place to help avoid these issues."

First, Harry explained each sprint offered a control level through the agile events (daily stand-up meeting, retrospective, demonstration, backlog refinement) occurring continuously throughout execution. For example, changes to requirements would only be addressed during new iteration planning. They would never interrupt the work being performed.

In addition to managing the product backlog in collaboration with Jim, Siwan would need to conduct a daily stand-up meeting, a short discussion, usually no more than 15-20 minutes in length, where every team member answers:

- What did I do yesterday to help the team meet our goals?
- What will my contributions be today?
- Is there anything that would prevent me from completing this work or from the team meeting our goals?

Harry continued with a brief story. "Some time ago, I worked with a company to assess its project management maturity. Management claimed they were running agile projects. One of the first things I asked about was the daily stand-up meeting."

"It turned out that the functional manager of development was conducting the meeting and only included the developers," Harry continued. "Testers, business analysts, product owners, and even the project manager were excluded. Without the benefit of the whole team together for problem-solving, work kept falling behind. Eventually, the failure to correct this led to both project and company failure."

Once everyone has a turn, the meeting ends. Any issues arising are discussed among the team in additional sessions, with only the involved individuals. The daily commitments help keep the team on task to complete all the stories and epics in the iteration. Interruptions from meetings are minimized and managed.

"There are some immediate benefits," continued Harry. "Since everyone on the team knows who is ahead and who is behind on their work, the team can work out the problem together. Best case, they could offer their assistance, and worst case, they could stay out of the way while those behind caught up. And since the meeting is kept short, it was an invaluable way to share the information."

At the end of each iteration, the team will self-evaluate their work in a retrospective meeting. A retrospective is a time when the reflects on the completion of an iteration and answers the following questions:

- What did we do well?
- What needs improvement?
- How will we work differently during the next iteration?

"Commitments made during the retrospective will require your follow up," Harry continued, "to be sure they are in place. After each retrospective, you will need to update the product backlog to remove completed stories and epics and analyze some critical metrics to control the iterations.

A burndown chart will track the metrics. A burndown chart is typically a bar chart plotting the progress of the story points in iterations."

The metrics requiring attention include:

- **Burn rate**: How many story points remain at the end of each day or this iteration? Story points are the points that were assigned during estimating. It helps us understand the rate at which work is completed and how much work is leftover after sprints.
- **Velocity**: At what rate is the team completing story points? Velocity helps us to understand the pace of the team. It is merely the number of story points for all fully completed stories in the sprint.
- **Value delivery**: How many valuable story points have been released to the client at this time? Did all the story contribute to the released functionality? Or perhaps some were to help position the product for future work?

Examining the burn rate and velocity will help the project manager determine how many story points should go into the next sprint. These may be referred to as Work in Progress (WIP) limits. Knowing how much work can be in each iteration will help determine when future releases might occur. The value delivery helps to assure the client that work is progressing. Deliveries should be easier to predict once the project has made some progress.

"Your initial reaction to the first sign of trouble in the metrics will be 'I've got to do something to correct that,'" said Harry. "While it is in our nature to want to solve problems, it's important not to overreact.

Some activities may be done early, and some may be done late. If everything is going smoothly, they will even out over time. On the other hand, if there is a trend – key metrics are missed over several iterations in a row – you will need to consider how to correct the issue best."

Some of the possibilities for correction include:

- **Wait longer** – see if the problem corrects itself
- **Take an action** – for example, ask someone to work overtime or ask someone else to help
- **Replan some other work** – postpone some work to happen in a follow up project or look for some unimportant work that can be eliminated
- **Consult with the product owner** – they will reserve the right to take other actions, such as to cancel or postpone the project for project features

---

"I have a Burndown Chart Template you can use to plot the metrics. Dennis and I will be here to support your decision-making process. If you take on more responsibilities in the future, these concepts will work for other project plans, such as budgets."

Next, Harry explained that Siwan had to master controlling requests for changes to her project, including the requirements, outputs, and deliverables: the project's scope.

Figure 12: Sample Burndown Chart

"Once the iterations begin, new requirements will be welcome at the start of each iteration. Invariably, agile projects require changes to the requirements. The best approach is to consider the change an opportunity."

"Capture all the information about the change. Carefully evaluate the change. How will it impact your plan? What stories or epics need to be changed or added in the product backlog? In which future sprint might it best be handled? Be sure that Jim, the product manager, is aware of the changes to the product backlog."

"What other things do I need to be concerned about to control the project?" Siwan inquired.

"Great question!" Harry responded. "Let's take a look at two more things."

First, the team should understand the 'definition of done.' This concept starts with user stories. The confirmations on the back of user story index cards should indicate any acceptance criteria. A story is done when implemented, meets all the requirements, passes all the acceptance criteria, and is accepted by the product owner.

Similarly, agile teams may define some stories, tasks, or other criteria that must be met for the result of an iteration to be releasable. Failure to meet these criteria at the end of an iteration will mean that the unfinished work will not be counted in the metrics toward completion.

Once work does meet the definition of done, the team needs to understand that it should not change anything without new user stories or the team's agreement. To do so risks breaking already completed work and adding more work to the project.

Limiting changes for finished work is especially important for software projects. It is not uncommon for developers to optimize or change the code to find that they break the existing functionality. Done is DONE!

Next, Harry posed a question, "Have you ever heard of Elmer Wheeler? At one time, he was America's top salesman. He is credited with the phrase 'Don't sell the steak, sell the sizzle!'"

"He had two other famous phrases that are applicable as well: 'Don't write – telegraph' and 'Watch your bark.' Each month you will need to provide a status report for Dennis and Movie Vault management." As he continued, Harry wrote on the whiteboard:

The 4 Rights of Status Reporting:

Right message, **R**ight time, **R**ight format, **R**ight people.

"Like Elmer, you want to telegraph – keep the messages short and concise. The first words are the most important."

"I've always sent Dennis a weekly status report but didn't pay too much attention to what I wrote," responded Siwan. "I've never heard of Elmer Wheeler."

"Elmer's sales tactics are still practiced today. A status report will help you maintain control because it keeps everyone informed about the project progress," continued Harry. "As Elmer would say, you also have to 'watch your bark' – consider the language you use."

"Because you are addressing people at all levels of the organizations involved in the project, be sure your messages are short, to the point, and easy to understand. Status reports are also an excellent opportunity to acknowledge and praise the team for a job well done – 'sell the sizzle.' Be sure to include successes and give credit to those who helped the team achieve them."

Harry continued to explain, "There is a tie-in with status reports and stakeholder analysis. Be sure to understand-upfront what the right time, the right message, the right format, and the right people are. You may also need to schedule face-to-face meetings with Movie Vault management or Dennis. Your communications should be detailed in the stakeholder register and communications plan, which we looked at during the first iteration."

"And one more thing," Harry continued. "Reviewing past status reports and other project information will help you to see if there are any trends or recurring issues of which you should be aware. These may include things like too much work consistently incomplete at the end of sprints. Incomplete sprints could indicate you should reduce the limit for future sprints.

"I'll provide you with a Status Report Template, but be aware it may require the most tailoring to be appropriate for your audience," cautioned Harry. "It is appropriate for Dennis, but other stakeholders, especially the team, may require more information."

Project Manager:	Swan Sero	Sponsor	Dennis Miller, Jim Curtis	Date:	11/20/2020
Project Progress Summary	Spradhita	Budget	N/A	Issues	10
	Summary: The project overall is making good progress. Some missing user stories were found when putting together the product backlog, but there are none affecting the current sprint and we will correct within the next two sprints.				
Project Milestones					
Milestone description	Expected date of completion	Status	Owner	Issues (yes/no)	Comments
Functional Requirements	10/16/2020	Completed	Swan	Yes	Missing user stories (10)
Product Backlog	10/30/2020	Completed	Jim, Swan, Team	Yes	See above
First sprint	11/20/2020	On-time	Jim, Swan, Team	No	
Project Risks and Issues					
Risks/Issues	Priority	Impact on project	Action		Owner
Missing User Stories	Medium	None expected	Swan is working on them		Swan
Sally taking vacation	Medium-High	Work of 3rd sprint may not be met	Adjusting sprints and milestone plan; per Jim, this won't be an issue		Swan
Budget					
Budget Spent (%)	N/A	Remaining (%)	N/A	Status	N/A
Sprint Metrics					
Burndown Rate:	Too early to measure	Velocity:	Too early to measure	Status	
Executive Assistance And Issue Escalations					
Assistance Needed/Issue Description		Action Requested			
None at this time		None at this time.			

Figure 13: Sample Status Report

"Now would be a good time to review the stakeholder register and communications plan and make sure these communications are included," continued Harry. "You also need to understand that any identified corrective actions used to set the project back on the right course must be sufficiently gentle so as not to oversteer."

"Have direct conversations with team members who are not meeting commitments. Let them know that there is an issue and ask for their help. Most good team members will take the opportunity to offer up suggestions for correction themselves. They may volunteer to put in some extra hours or suggest they can come in on a day off. Let them choose how they will fix the issue. You should discuss with Jim and Dennis at what point they want to hear about this information."

"It's also important to minimize the work associated with status reports. Since you will be leading the daily stand-up meetings, you will have a pretty good idea of status. Minimize the time you ask others for help in producing this report. Project controls in excess may themselves derail a project. Each project control consumes time and resources. So carefully evaluate how you want to expend that time and budget."

"What should I do if a bigger correction is needed?" inquired Siwan.

"If a larger correction is necessary, be sure to involve the team. More heads are better than one," continued Harry. "Together, the team will often find a solution. Empower team members to do it. You are there to coach and mentor if they get stuck or cannot find a suitable path. And if you are unable to, Dennis and I are here to support you."

"But what if a team member isn't forthcoming about an issue?" Siwan inquired.

"By keeping in regular contact with the team, that will be difficult for someone to do. If it does happen, be sure the team member knows they are accountable for their work and actions."

"Concealing an issue is not acceptable," explained Harry. "You need to be sure everyone knows that the best project environment is where there is a lot of open, transparent communication and collaboration. It's OK to discuss issues and make mistakes. Have them think of mistakes as learning opportunities."

"Remember the company that had developers only at the daily stand-up meeting? Another problem leading to their demise was the lack of transparent communication. No one on the management team wanted to hear about issues, so there was limited participation in finding a resolution. Further, even when they were provided with potential resolutions, management continued to ignore the issues, leading to a fairly toxic working environment with diminishing success."

As the Monday drew to a close and the project start date was only two days away, Harry asked Siwan to summarize this time. She included:

Chapter Summary

- C is for control.
- The short nature and structure of the iterations are primary controls.
  - Daily stand-up meetings
  - Retrospectives
  - Demonstrations
  - Backlog revisions
  - Work in Progress limits
  - Definition of done
  - Metrics and Burndown Charts
- Be sure control is casual – don't oversteer or overreact. You can:
  - Wait a little longer
  - Take a small action
  - Replan some of the work
  - Consult with the product owner
- Master change control
  - New requirements acceptable at the start of an iteration
  - Definition of done – no changes to completed work
  - Only the work in the product backlog is considered
- Regular status reports
  - Short and concise
  - Tailored to the audience
  - Consider the language used
  - Successes and recognition
  - Review for trends or recurring issues
- Flexible and Gentle Steering
  - Don't oversteer
  - Control controls – they expend resources

- o Empower the team to find solutions with transparent and open communications
- Tools and templates
  - o Burndown Chart Template
  - o Status Report Template
  - o Agile Events
  - o Work in Progress Limits
  - o Definition of Done

"Good job, Siwan!" Harry exclaimed. "You understand the basics of control. Tomorrow is our last day together before the project begins, so try to relax these next two evenings."

Knowledge Nuggets

Chapter Pro Tip: Compile useful information as you go.

Projects generate vast amounts of data beyond the regular retrospectives and lessons learned. As the project progresses, collect, index, and even diarize this data.

Project data and documents contain information such as:

- Plans and changes to plans (e.g., to the product backlog)
- Performance of the project and people involved (save the metrics)
- Value and benefits the project provided (value delivery)
- Problems faced and decisions made (retrospectives and lessons learned)
- Value-added ideas for the future of the project
- Memorable things people said

This level of historical data may not only help in future projects and learning. It may boost your career with valuable information you might otherwise forget.

Agile Practice Guide reading: Section 5.2 covers agile events; section 5.4 covers metrics in agile projects.

PMBOK® Guide reading: As a process, monitoring and controlling occur throughout all the knowledge areas. Refer to Table 1-4 for the specific sections.

Chapter Templates: Burndown Chart, Status Report

CHAPTER 7

ITERATION 7: TRANSFER

It was now Tuesday morning and the seventh iteration of her preparation. Siwan knew that tomorrow the project would start, and she felt that Harry had prepared her well. They had one last day together, and she was ready to make the most of it. Harry wasn't in her office, but she found him in the conference room, writing on the board:

Every project is an opportunity to learn, to solve problems, to embrace opportunities, and to transform the team.

"Good morning, Siwan," started Harry as he turned around. "Just as Olympic gymnasts have to 'stick' their landings, project managers need to bring their projects to a successful conclusion and learn from the successes and failures along the way. The intermediate deliverables of working software are less significant, but you will be remembered for the final product delivery. Today we're going to talk about T for Transfer to prepare you to 'stick' your project's landing."

"Harry, I'm feeling prepared and want to thank you for all you've done to help me. I've learned a lot, and I'm going to do my best not to disappoint anyone," stated Siwan.

"You're welcome, Siwan," Harry continued. "It's my pleasure. Getting the project successfully into user and client hands is what most people will remember the project manager for, so this is very important."

"I worked with a project manager a long time ago that had not learned this lesson. The project was to develop a reporting application for a client that sold a software service to their clients. The goal was to produce the reports on the first day of each month. The application had both development and testing issues, and then was put into production without proper planning."

"What kind of impact did that have?" inquired Siwan.

Harry explained that the reports were delivered on the first of each month, but one full month late. Support staff was sleeping under their desks to restart the application, which would fail frequently and need to be restarted. The team invited Harry to help solve the problem, and he found a simple answer.

Rather than restart from the beginning, the output was saved. The process could pick up where it left off, and after the reset, new data could be appended to the existing data. The fix took only six lines of code! Now the reports came close enough to the first of the month that the developers could make some optimizations to meet the goal completely. With the application's chaotic transfer, including serious issues, the application was not acceptable to the client.

"Siwan, when you transfer the final product to Movie Vault to put into production, you need to make sure everything is in order and delivered per the agreed requirements. They need to get the 'white glove, red carpet' treatment – they will feel good not just about the product but also about you and your team at Xanadu. To achieve a high level of satisfaction requires attention to many details:

- Any known issues from thorough testing are documented, including any workarounds.
- Schedule a meeting with Jim and his team from Movie Vault to demonstrate the product and officially turn over its operation.
- The demonstration reflects the Movie Vault acceptance criteria and tests for the project.
- Use the meeting to ask Jim and his team if there are any other tests they may want to have performed.
- Plan to have a full user acceptance test and document the results before the project's final transfer occurs.
- Final requirements, training documentation, user guides, operational information such as roles, user names, passwords, and other documents should be ready for Jim and his team and provided at that meeting.
- You and your team will support Jim and his team as needed for the first few weeks until they are comfortable. After that, support becomes the responsibility of the Movie Vault support team.
- You consult with Dennis to find out if there are any other requirements he or Xanadu has to complete the project."

"At this point, a complete and professional transfer will help to get Jim and his team up to speed and prepare them to sign off on your project. This process will take less effort since they have had incremental deliveries, but it is nonetheless important."

"I can do that," Siwan added confidently. "I'll make sure that the tasks of our testing, user acceptance testing, and documentation are also in the milestone plan."

PROJECT MANAGERS AND ETHICS

Project management involves people - people making a lot of decisions, some of which revolve around ethical dilemmas and difficult choices.

Ethics is about doing things right. Ethical decision making, trust, and integrity all contribute to high performing teams and leaders.

"That's how to do it," encouraged Harry. "All the work needs to be in the plan, so there are no last-minute scrambles to accomplish work that wasn't in the plan."

"You will also need to measure your delivery. Suppose Movie Vault sets a goal that purchase transactions need to complete in under ten seconds. In that case, you will need to measure performance to ensure the requirement is met. You should go back to all the requirements which are measurable and make sure the product meets all their goals."

"I'll make sure that also gets into the plan. What should we do, for example, if we are close to the goals but not quite meeting them?" Siwan inquired.

"Honesty and transparency with a client are the best approaches when a goal has not been completely met," Harry stated. "Inform Jim at Movie Vault as soon as you discover any performance or other limitations. You want to get his feedback in advance, if possible, in case major changes to the requirements, scope, or product need to be made."

"If you can get the performance to 13 seconds instead of ten, determine what it will take to get to ten. Always remember to think about scope, time, cost, and resources. When your analysis is complete, review the results with Dennis and Jim. Movie Vault may agree to accept the application if there is a plan in place to meet the goal shortly after delivery. Alternatively, if you can demonstrate why it might not be possible or too expensive to reach, they may also accept it. You don't want to promise ten and have them discover it is 13 after they accepted the delivery. You should demonstrate integrity and ethics throughout the process."

After Siwan had a few minutes to think about their discussion and jot down a few notes about the closeout planning required, Harry continued. "Siwan, if you establish yourself as having basic management skills, your career at Xanadu will be on the rise. In practice, Dennis should evaluate the team. But he won't be working with them on a day-to-day basis as you. As part of the project wrap up you should write short evaluations for each team member."

"I'll provide a Team Member Evaluation Template, which will stress both accomplishments and areas for development. I know Dennis will appreciate the information. The project manager for your last project did this – it's how you were identified for this opportunity."

Team Member	John Smith		Project Manager	Siwan Sero
Strengths and Achievements	Area for Improvement		Proposed Action	Comments
Supported the project goals and objectives. Always communicated clearly and participated in giving frequent feedback to improve results. Solved a complex reporting module performance issue and improved module performance by 10%. Demonstrated leadership by assuming more responsibility for the reporting module and the administrative module.	Needs some improvements in problem-solving methodology in order to provide efficient reporting results and follow a standardized problem-solving strategy.		Allocate time for training in problem-solving and decision making. Nominate for quarterly Xanadu management award.	Supporting form and documentation attached.

Figure 14: Sample Team Member Evaluation

"There is one last item we need to work on – lessons learned," stated Harry. "Siwan, thinking about how we spent our time together over the last seven days, what worked best for you?"

111

"Well, to start with," Siwan began thoughtfully, "I liked how the time was structured. You had stories from real experiences and situations which illustrated the points. Then, we did a deeper dive into the specific areas. And at the end of each iteration, you summarized the learning. The variety of meeting locations and some of the 'homework' assignments also helped make everything more memorable. The PROJECT methodology is going to be very hard to forget based on how its presentation."

"Excellent!" exclaimed Harry pleased that his mentee was doing well and, most of all, learning. "What do you think could be improved?" he asked next.

"That's a little harder to answer right now," Siwan said. "Everything seemed to go very well. I just wish there was time for more practice of the concepts. But the templates you are providing will help, and I'm willing to put in the extra effort as the project gets underway."

"Outstanding," stated Harry. "I will consider adding more practice to my presentations. I may even document everything in a book, so other clients like you will be able to refer back to concepts and review them as the project progresses."

"What we just accomplished, Siwan, is how lessons learned can be completed simply for your project," said Harry as he jotted down on the board:

- Ask what was done well and worth repeating
- Ask what needs improvement for the next time, or perhaps that we shouldn't do any more
- Share with Dennis so he can share with the other managers to immediately put plans in place to act on the feedback for the next project
- Use the feedback to improve your delivery of the next project
- Continue to work as necessary to integrate the changes into your routine and that of other Xanadu project managers

Too many project managers skip this step, stating a lack of time. Many agile projects ignore it as well, thinking the retrospectives covered everything. The retrospectives may contribute to the lessons learned. Still, there may be some other lessons spanning the retrospectives or for different phases of the project. But including our discussions, how long did this take?"

Siwan thought for a moment and saw Harry's point: conducting a lessons learned meeting does not have to take a lot of time or create more overhead. In a little less than an hour, Siwan provided feedback to Harry, and he was prepared to act on it in the future.

"Less than an hour, so it didn't take a lot of time," she stated out loud. "I think this might be a good way to implement continuous improvement in project management."

"Exactly, Siwan," said Harry. "And you don't have to wait until the end of the project. You might work with the team to gather lessons learned after each project phase or after some major deliverables have been completed. I'll provide a Lessons Learned

Template, which will help organize the information and remind you of the opportunities to collect it."

Successes	Detailed description	Project Impact	Suggested improvements
Early completion of Movie Vault login screen	Due to some reusable code, the team was able to finish the login screen programming early and accomplish more work in the sprint	Helped us to move those programmers to another task that was falling behind	Always look for reusable code

Areas for improvements	Detailed description	Project Impact	Suggested Actions
Overall project estimation	Work of sprints often didn't complete on time because sizing estimates/story points were not good.	Made it difficult as we had to move around resources to complete tasks on time constantly.	Estimation training to improve Planning Poker practices.

Figure 15: Sample Lessons Learned

"After the failure of the reporting project that I spoke of earlier today, I convinced the project manager and management of the company that they needed to improve a lot of things. Rather than do everything at once, we made a list and prioritized it. With each new project, they continued to add and prioritize and implement items on the list."

"I also developed the templates overtime for them. Their project manager tailored them for their specific projects. Their next projects were far more successful, and they managed to repair the relationship with the client."

So, as he did the previous iteration, Harry asked Siwan to summarize what they discussed and learned together that day:

Chapter Summary

- T is for transfer
  - Transfer the project to the client
  - Transform the team through evaluations and lessons learned
- Treat the client with white gloves
  - Transfer thoroughly tested product, including client acceptance test results
  - Meet with the client for turnover, including demonstration
  - Provide training and all documentation
  - Provide excellent support to see the client through the transition
- Measure Your Delivery
  - Meet client requirements and other expectations for performance
  - Measure performance whenever possible
  - Facts and negotiation with the client may help
  - Demonstrate integrity and ethics for best results
- Team Evaluations
  - Short feedback document
  - Stress accomplishments and development needs
  - Provide to management without any expectations
- Lessons Learned
  - What worked well
  - What needs improvement
  - How will we act on this for the next project(s)?
- Tools and templates
  - Team Member Evaluation Template
  - Lessons Learned Template

Before departing for the day, Siwan and Harry spent some time reviewing each of the daily summaries. Harry helped fill in some gaps. In just seven days, seven iterations, Siwan learned the basics of proper project management to succeed. She left feeling confident that she would be ready to start the project the next day.

Chapter Pro Tip: Do the right thing, even when no one asks or is watching.

Ethics is about doing the right things. When you have integrity, you will continue to do them, even when no one is watching.

What if your manager is forcing you to do something unethical? The best advice is to stand your ground and find a new job (or manager) if necessary.

Projects can be full of ethical dilemmas – the hard choices we must make. These occur many times in project management, as management or stakeholders' pressure you or the team to:

- Produce incomplete reports, half-truths, and lies with statistics
- Skew results "just a little"
- Delay reporting to avoid harmful data or emphasize positive data
- Develop scapegoats – who to blame for poor results
- Emphasize one area to prevent scrutiny of another
- Report positive or negative progress not supported by data
- Make unapproved changes or "gold plate" the project
- Not exercise due care – not follow processes

As you make choices and have possible solutions and decisions, consider the following questions:

- Am I feeling pressured to decide one way or the other?

- Does the decision meet requirements, is it legal, and does it conform with all regulatory requirements and policies?
- Is it fair and balanced for everyone concerned?
- How will I feel about myself once I go home?

Keep in mind that trust and integrity are essential to teamwork and maintaining your ability to manage by influence. Once an unethical behavior is uncovered, it is difficult to regain the trust you need to succeed.

PMBOK® Guide reading: Section 1, Chapter 4.7 covers the project closeout process; for more information about ethics, visit https://www.pmi.org/ethics.

Chapter Templates: Team Member Evaluation, Lessons Learned

CHAPTER **8**

EPILOGUE

Wednesday morning, Siwan was at Xanadu bright and early. She had several appointments already scheduled over the next few days to begin stakeholder identification and find out about the project's internal expectations. The following week she would head to Movie Vault to start the elicitation of requirements. As she neared the end of elicitation, she sent Dennis her suggestions for team members and scheduled the kickoff meeting.

Siwan had copious notes to review, templates to modify and fill out, meetings to schedule, and plans to be made after her consultation with Harry. In their short time together, Siwan and Harry learned from each other. Siwan was pleased with the result and confident she would be able to manage the project.

As the project progressed, Siwan kept reviewing the PROJECT methodology and using the templates that Harry provided. Rather than just use them as-is, she carefully examined and modified them as needed for the project, satisfying both Xanadu's and Clark Inc.'s needs specific to the project. These steps helped her tremendously, as the project would not be without issues. As promised, Harry and Dennis were available to help her clear roadblocks, listen to problems she had in making decisions, and provide other support as required.

As a result of her preparation, Siwan successfully navigated through some of the more challenging aspects of project management:

- The team did a more thorough job identifying stakeholders, gathering requirements, and completing the initial product backlog
- The team, client, and other stakeholders always knew what had to be done next
- Even with the uncertainty created by the agile life cycle's use, the project completed and met all of Jim's expectations.
- Siwan regularly met with team members and provided feedback
- Follow up on critical assignments and delegations happened daily
- Siwan provided regular project progress updates to the client and Xanadu leadership team
- Team members weren't just accountable for their work – they took pride in it
- As she wrote evaluations, Siwan beamed with pride as everyone performed well
- Siwan maintained the visibility of the project, which also helped to motivate the team

As the project was well under control, Siwan began studying the many project topics that Harry wasn't able to include in his seven-iteration preparation, including:

- Schedule network diagrams for project timelines
- Basics of budgeting and finance
- Earned value management systems
- Advanced estimation techniques

- Advanced risk management processes and tools
- Organizational structures and management theory
- Procurement documents and processes
- Basic tools of quality
- A full treatment of all the processes, including project initiation, full scope, risk, and change management
- Additional soft skills, such as negotiation and conflict resolution.

The Movie Vault project completed in less than a year as the client expected and was considered an enormous success, both by the client and Xanadu.

In between projects, Siwan continued to build her knowledge of project management and more advanced project management tools like Microsoft® Teams, monday.com, and Microsoft® Project®. After she completed a few more projects, the company grew, and a new management position opened – guess who filled it?

The opening occurred because Dennis moved up in the organization. He recognized that it would be difficult for Siwan if she didn't have training and mentors. And the success that she created with that approach helped to earn her a place in senior management.

After a long and successful career as a project manager and project management consultant, Harry memorialized the PROJECT methodology in a book. He and Heda headed to a tropical beach in parts of the world unknown. He was satisfied that through his writing, he could help accidental agile project managers like Siwan to:

- Become heroes in their organizations by succeeding with their projects

- Master the easy basics of agile project management
- Build credibility as project managers
- Use the advice, tools, and templates to make sound decisions for their projects
- Identify future learning goals and needs
- Get on a path for potential certifications such as Certified Scrum Master (CSM), PMI-ACP (Agile Certified Practitioner), and DA (Disciplined Agile has multiple certifications)
- Start building long term careers

Do you know someone who is or is about to become an accidental agile project manager? Do them a favor and share Siwan's story with them.

FIN

Author's Notes

The templates referenced in this book (as well as other PPC Group, LLC publications) are available "as is." You may download them and change them for your use. To access them, please visit accidentalpm.online/downloads.

Once registered, you will receive an email with your account information. The contents will also be in your online library. For any issues, please contact support@ppcgroup.us.

The following tables show the skills included in this book. Although referred to as a "quick start" guide, this book, directly and indirectly, touches on a large number of skills and knowledge areas.

Project management is a journey, not a destination. There is no easy way to absorb all the skills and knowledge required in a term or semester, let alone seven days or iterations. By starting and focusing on fundamentals, readers will gain a rock-solid foundation. There is plenty of time to learn the more advanced topics not covered in this book. Think of it as your continuous improvement.

Keep in mind that the PMP® Exam requires at least three years of work in project management. The need for experience gives you time to learn more advanced skills, like Earned Value and Network Diagrams.

You can show progress by earning a Project Hero social badge through our course, Accidental Project Manager: The Online Experience. We are also creating a new online class, Accidental Agile Project Manager: The Online Experience. You can also study and prepare for a CAPM® (Certified Associate Project Manager) certification. This certification has no experience need. Our Project Hero Academy is your roadmap to project management success.

Primary Competency	Sub-competency	Book Coverage
Know-how	Domain Know-how	*These are the subject matter, industry, and organizational specific skills learned in normal career development and on the job.*
	Technical Know-how	
	Process Know-how	
	Financial Management Know-How	
Personal Excellence	Negotiation	Not covered
	Integrity and Ethics	√
	Respect for individual	Indirect
	Attitude & Perseverance	Indirect
Team / Internal Stakeholders Management	Leadership	√
	Oral Communication	√
	Written Communication	√
	Delegation	√
	Team Management	√
	Networking & Collaboration	Collaboration √ Networking - Indirect
	Accountability	√
	Managing Conflict	Not covered
Thinking Skills	Problem Solving & Decision Making	Indirect
	Analytical Thinking	Indirect
	Innovative/Creative Thinking	Not covered
	Questioning/Probing	Indirect
Customer Management	Cross-Cultural Competency	√
	Customer Awareness	Indirect
	Oral Communication	Indirect
	Written Communication	Indirect

Project Management Knowledge	Integration Management	√
	Scope Management	√
	Schedule Management	√
	Cost Management	Not covered
	Quality Management	Not covered
	Resource Management	√
	Communication Management	√
	Risk Management	Indirect
	Procurement Management	Not covered
	Stakeholder Management	√
Project Management Processes	Initiating	Not covered
	Planning	√
	Executing	√
	Monitoring & Controlling	√
	Closing	√

Table 4: Coverage of Project Management Competencies from the *PMBOK® Guide*

PROJECT Methodology Step	Agile and Project Management Concepts Included
Introduction	Definitions of project, operations, project manager Agile principles Project life cycles
People	Agile team descriptions, roles, and responsibilities Cross-functional teams Stakeholder identification and management Communications management
Requirements	User stories and epics Requirements elicitation techniques (interviews, observation, document review) Collaboration
Organize	Agile estimating (tee-shirt sizing, planning poker Product backlog Product roadmap Iterations in the milestone plan
Jell	Agile team descriptions, roles, and responsibilities Cross-functional teams Virtual teams Team formation Teambuilding
Execute	Iterations Agile events (stand-up meeting, retrospectives, demonstrations, backlog refinement) Delegation Follow up Feedback Accountability Collaboration
Control	Agile events (stand-up meeting, retrospectives, demonstrations, backlog refinement) Work in Progress (WIP) Limit Definition of done

	Burndown charts
	Status reports
Transfer	Demonstrations
	Client turnover meetings
	Team evaluation
	Lessons learned

Table 5: Mapping of Agile and Project Management Concepts to the PROJECT Management Method

References

Agile Business Consortium Content Team. "Chapter 10: Moscow Prioritisation." DSDM Agile Project Framework Handbook. Agile Business Consortium, 2019. https://www.agilebusiness.org/page/ProjectFramework_10_MoSCoWPrioritisation.

Andersen, E.S. "Milestone Planning—a Different Planning Approach." Bangkok, Thailand, 2006. https://www.pmi.org/learning/library/milestone-different-planning-approach-7635.

Anderson Economic Group. *Project Management Job Growth and Talent Gap 2017-2027.* Project Management Institute, 2017. https://www.pmi.org/-/media/pmi/documents/public/pdf/learning/job-growth-report.pdf.

Bailey, Sebastian. "How to Overcome the Five Major Disadvantages of Virtual Working." *Forbes.* https://www.forbes.com/sites/sebastianbailey/2013/03/05/how-to-overcome-the-five-major-disadvantages-of-virtual-working/#28aff5d62734.

Baker, E. "Planning Effective Stakeholder Management Strategies to Do the Same Thing!" Vancouver, BC: Project Management Institute, 2012. https://www.pmi.org/learning/library/planning-effective-stakeholder-management-strategies-development-6058.

Beck, Kent et al. "Manifesto for Agile Software Development." Manifesto for Agile Software Development, 2001. https://agilemanifesto.org.

Buffett, Mary, and David Clark. *Warren Buffett's Management Secrets: Proven Tools for Personal and Business Success.* 1st Scribner hardcover ed. New York: Scribner, 2009.

Carpenter, Mark. "What are Agile Ceremonies?" *Clearly Agile Blog.* (blog), 2018. https://www.clearlyagileinc.com/agile-blog/what-are-agile-ceremonies.

Cohn, Michael. "Estimating with T-Shirt Sizes." *Mike Cohn's Blog at Mountain Goat Software* (blog). Mountain Goat Software, 2013. https://www.mountaingoatsoftware.com/blog/estimating-with-tee-shirt-sizes.

———. "User Stories and User Story Examples by Mike Cohn." Mountain Goat Software. https://www.mountaingoatsoftware.com/agile/user-stories.

Crowe, Andy. *Alpha Project Managers: What the Top 2% Know That Everyone Else Does Not.* Place of publication not identified: Velociteach, 2016.

Forman, J. B., and R. Discenza. "Got Stake?: (Holder) Management in Your Project." Vancouver, BC: Project Management Institute, 2012. https://www.pmi.org/learning/library/stakeholder-management-plan-6090.

Frohnhoefer, Ray. "Plan Projects Like Albert Einstein." *Project Hero Blog* (blog), 2019a. https://www.accidentalpm.online/blog/plan-projects-like-albert-einstein.

———. *Risk Assessment Framework: Successfully Navigating Uncertainty.* 2nd ed. San Diego, CA: PPC Group, LLC, 2019b.

———. "Communicate, Communicate, Communicate ." *Project Hero Blog* (blog), 2020a. https://www.accidentalpm.online/blog/communicate-communicate-communicate.

———. "You Know You Are a 'Knighted' Project Manager When …." *Project Hero Blog* (blog), 2020b. https://www.accidentalpm.online/blog/you-know-you-are-a-knighted-project-manager-when.

Fuqua, Anthony. "How Many Stories Per Sprint? Rules of Thumb." *Leading Agile Blog* (blog), 2015. https://www.leadingagile.com/2015/05/how-many-user-stories-per-sprint-rules-of-thumb/.

Haus, Marian. "Are Your Communication Habits Good Enough?" *Voices on Project Management Blog* (blog), 2016.

https://www.projectmanagement.com/blog-post/18979/Are-Your-Communication-Habits-Good-Enough--.

Hossenlopp, Rosemary, and Kathleen B. Hass. *Unearthing Business Requirements: Elicitation Tools and Techniques*. Business Analysis Essential Library. Vienna, VA: Management Concepts, 2008.

Hunsberger, K. "The Accidental Project Manager." *PM Network*, 2011.

Jeffries, Ron. "Essential XP: Card, Conversation, Confirmation." *Ron Jeffries* (blog), 2001. https://ronjeffries.com/xprog/articles/expcardconversationconfirmation

Jordan, A. "Project Manager Accountability." *Voices on Project Management Blog* (blog), 2017. https://www.projectmanagement.com/articles/406759/Project-Manager-Accountability.

Larson, E. "I Don't Have Time to Manage Requirements: My Project Is Late Already." Phoenix, AZ: Project Management Institute, 2008. https://www.pmi.org/learning/library/time-manage-requirements-project-late-6956.

Lewis, Richard. "How Different Cultures Understand Time." *Business Insider*, 2014. http://www.businessinsider.com/how-different-cultures-understand-time-2014-5.

Mind Tools Content Team. "How Well Do You Delegate? Discover Ways to Achieve More." MindTools, 2018. https://www.mindtools.com/pages/article/newTMM_60.htm.

———. "Servant Leadership" MindTools, n.d., https://www.mindtools.com/pages/article/servant-leadership.htm

Mountain Goat Software. "Planning Poker," 2020. https://www.mountaingoatsoftware.com/agile/planning-poker.

Project Management Institute, ed. *A Guide to the Project Management Body of Knowledge (PMBOK Guide)*. Sixth edition. Newtown

Square, Pennsylvania: Project Management Institute, Inc, 2017a.

———, ed. *The Agile Practice Guide.* Newtown Square, Pennsylvania: The Project Management Institute, 2017b.

Pulsifer, Simon et al. "Panama Canal." Wikipedia. Wikimedia Foundation, 2018. https://en.wikipedia.org/wiki/Panama_Canal.

Reina, Michelle, Dennis Reina, and David Hudnut. "Why Trust Is Critical to Team Success." Research Report. Center for Creative Leadership, 2017. https://www.ccl.org/wp-content/uploads/2017/05/why-trust-is-critical-team-success-research-report.pdf.

Shore, James, and Shane Warden. *The Art of Agile Development.* Theory in Practice. Sebastopol, CA: O'Reilly Media, Inc, 2008.

The Teambuilding Directory Content Team. "The Team Building Directory - Dream Trip." The Teambuilding Directory, 2018. http://www.innovativeteambuilding.co.uk/activity/dream-trip/.

Umlas, Judith W. *The Power of Acknowledgment.* New York: IIL Pub., 2006.

Index

133

134

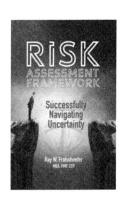

Accidental Project Manager:
The Online Experience

PLAN TO MANAGE PROJECTS SUCCESSFULLY!

- Learn the fundamental concepts and terms
- Take the training anywhere, anytime, on any device
- Earn a Project Hero social badge from Accredible

If you are an aspiring, new, or accidental project manager, this course, which goes beyond the book, is for you. Your instructor has over 20 years of project management experience and has two Amazon international best-selling books on project management.

Upon completing the course and spending at least 23 hours engaged with it, you will earn your Project Hero social badge from Accredible. You also meet your training requirement for the CAPM® certification.

While you may complete the course in as few as seven days, you will have access for six months. During this time, you will have access to any changes, updates, upgrades, and new materials added during that time. You keep all downloaded materials.

As a valued reader, you can access the course for 50% off. Visit https://www.accidentalpm.online/apm-online-course-offer for details.

As a valued reader, you have access to all the templates referenced in this book and those accompanying our other books!

Sign up for access (you keep the downloads, plus they are in your online library) at:

accidentalpm.online/downloads

Bonus: Our PM Best Practices and Tips will be delivered once a month to your inbox.

Printed in Great Britain
by Amazon